Relax with

CHESS

AND WIN IN 20 MOVES

by FRED REINFELD

PITMAN PUBLISHING CORPORATION

NEW YORK   LONDON

First Published 1948

Associated Companies
SIR ISAAC PITMAN & SONS, LTD.
LONDON   MELBOURNE   JOHANNESBURG   GENEVA

SIR ISAAC PITMAN & SONS (CANADA), LTD.
TORONTO

CONTENTS

THE RECORDING OF CHESS GAMES

CHESS NOTATION IS easy to learn. It is indispensable to every chess player: familiarity with chess notation increases your capacity for enjoyment of the game, and your ability to improve your play.

The notation is made easy and rapid by the use of commonsense symbols, thus:

King	K	Pawn	P
Queen	Q	check	*ch*
Rook	R	captures	×
Knight	Kt	good move	*!*
Bishop	B	bad move	*?*
castles King-side		O–O	
castles Queen-side		O–O–O	

All chess notations are based on a combination of two factors: *the name of the piece that is moved, and the name of the square to which it is moved.*

Some readers will be surprised to learn that the squares have names! By way of learning (or reviewing) the chess notation, let us play over an entertaining little game.

The next column shows the opening position (in chess diagrams, the *White* Pawns move toward the *top* of the page; the *Black* Pawns move toward the bottom of the page).

The vertical rows of squares (running from top to bottom) are called *files*. They are named after the pieces which stand on them at the beginning of the game. The file on which the Kings stand is therefore known as the King file.

The Pawns are named after the file in which they stand. Thus, the Pawn in front of each King is known as the King's Pawn.

The horizontal rows of squares (running from side to side), are known as *ranks*. White's back row (nearest to the bottom of the page) is called his *first rank*. His King is said to stand on K1; his Queen is on Q1.

The row on which the Pawns stand at the beginning of the game is White's second rank. Thus, his King's Pawn stands on K2; his Queen's Pawn on Q2.

The Bishop next to the King is called the King's Bishop and stands on KB1. The King's Knight stands on KKt1. The Queen's Rook (the Rook nearest to the Queen) stands on QR1.

Note this: if the King's Pawn advances two squares, it is now on K4. Note also that Black numbers *his* moves from *his* side of the board.

Now we are ready to play:

WHITE	BLACK
1 P–K4	P–K4

Make these moves using your own board and men; then check the resulting position with the following diagram:

Now each side brings out a Knight:

2 Kt–KB3   Kt–QB3

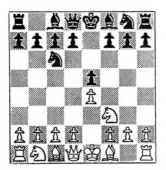

That was a bit harder than the Pawn moves, wasn't it?! Now let's try two moves on each side before we use a diagram:

3 B–Kt5	B–B4
4 P–B3	Kt–B3

Now we get our first captures, as well as our first example of castling:

5 B × Kt   QP × B

Note that it is the *Queen's Pawn* which recaptures!

6 O–O   B–KKt5

[2]

All right so far? We proceed:

7 P–KR3 P–KR4*!?*

Is this move good or bad? We don't know—it's a bit of both!

8 P×B P×P
9 Kt×P P–Kt6*!*

That one was a stinger—definitely good!

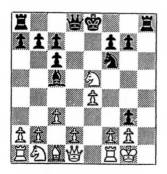

10 P–Q4 Kt×P*!*

Now he threatens 11 ... R–R8*ch!*; 12 K×R, Q–R5*ch* and mate next move!

11 Q–Kt4 B×P

11 ... P×P*ch!* would have won at once. Can you see how?!

12 Q×Kt B×P*ch*

White resigns, for if 13 R×B, Q–Q8*ch*; 14 Q–K1, Q×Q*ch*; 15 R–B1, R–R8*ch*; 16 K×R, Q×R *mate*.

This game, played at Berlin about 1851, was won by Anderssen against Mayet. At move 11, Black could have won by 11 ... P×P*ch*; 12 R×P, R–R8*ch!*; 13 K×R, Kt×R*ch* winning the Queen.

You can now proceed with the games in the text.

[3]

FIXED IDEAS

THE STORY GOES that a practical joker, taking advantage of Akiba Rubinstein's predilection for 1 P–Q4, once nailed down the grandmaster's Queen's Pawn. What appears as a harmless foible in a great player may, however, be magnified to dangerous proportions in his weaker brethren.

It is this quality which spoils so many Morphy games for us. His opponents always "attacked"; always defended badly, if at all; always underestimated the problem of defense—insofar as they were aware of it.

TWO KNIGHTS'
DEFENSE

(*Remove White's Queen's Rook*)

New Orleans, 1858

[After 18 O–O mate!]

WHITE	BLACK
P. *Morphy*	*Amateur*
1 P–K4	P–K4
2 Kt–KB3	Kt–QB3
3 B–B4	Kt–B3
4 Kt–Kt5	P–Q4
5 P×P	Kt×P [*a*]
6 Kt×BP?!	K×Kt
7 Q–B3*ch*	K–K3
8 Kt–B3	Kt–Q5? [*b*]
9 B×Kt*ch*	K–Q3
10 Q–B7	B–K3? [*c*]
11 B×B	Kt×B
12 Kt–K4*ch*	K–Q4

13 P–B4*ch!*	K×Kt [*d*]
14 Q×Kt	Q–Q5? [*e*]
15 Q–Kt4*ch*	K–Q6
16 Q–K2*ch* [*f*]	K–B7
17 P–Q3*ch!*	K×B [*g*]
18 O–O *mate!* [*h*]*	

[4]

[a] Objectively this is not a blunder, since White's sacrificial reply (the " Fried Liver") is unsound against the best defense. But since Black is patently incapable of playing the best defense, he should content himself with the more prudent 5 ... Kt–QR4 (see Field–Tenner, page 76).

[b] He leaves his menaced Knight in the lurch, and prefers " attack." Even this inferior move is permissible at the odds, but best of all is 8 ... Kt–K2 (unsatisfactory when White has his Queen's Rook).

[c] A much better reply to the threatened 11 Kt–K4 mate is 10 ... Q–K2! forcing White to retreat without adequate compensation for the Rook minus.

[d] He must bite into the sour apple, for after 13 ... K–B3; 14 Q×Kt ch, B–Q3; 14 Q–Q5 ch, K–Q2; 15 P–B5 (15 Kt–B5 ch?, K–K1!) White is ahead in material and has a winning attack to boot.

[e] If 14 ... Q–B3; 15 Q–Kt4 ch, K–Q6 (or 15 ... Q–B5; 16 P–Q3 ch); 16 Q–K2 ch as in the game. But 14 ... K–Q5! was a far better defensive try.

[f] Morphy makes chess seem very simple. The contrast between his elegant economy and Black's ineffectual bumbling is quite vivid: the Black monarch is forced into a fantastic mating net.

[g] Even refusal would have been unavailing: 17 ... K–Kt8; 18 O–O, K×P; 19 Q–B2! and Black is helpless against the coming discovered check with the QKtP.

[h] Morphy resolutely refused to allow his opponent's weak play to cheat him of a fine finish.

THE PRICE OF PROGRESS

INCREASED KNOWLEDGE must be paid for with disenchantment. Specifically, as applied to chess, this means that many a pretty combination of the old masters fails to stand up under the searching scrutiny of modern analysis.

It would be sheer perversity, however, to dismiss such combinations because of their flaws. Most of these flashy sacrifices were improvised under "skittles" conditions; it would be captious to expect perfection from them, or to pout because they do not meet the most rigid specifications.

GIUOCO PIANO
Philadelphia, 1860

[After 10 Kt–KB3]

	WHITE	BLACK
	Amateur	*G. Derrickson*
1	P–K4	P–K4
2	B–B4	Kt–KB3
3	Kt–KB3	Kt–B3
4	O–O	B–B4 [a]
5	P–Q3	P–Q3
6	B–KKt5 [b]	B–KKt5
7	P–KR3	P–KR4?!
8	P×B [c]	P×P
9	Kt–R2	P–Kt6
10	Kt–KB3 [d]*	Kt–KKt5?!
11	B×Q? [e]	B×Pch [f]
12	R×B	P×Rch
13	K–B1	R–R8ch

14	K–K2	R×Q
15	KKt–Q2 [g]	Kt–Q5ch!!
16	K×R	Kt–K6ch
17	K–B1	Kt–K7 *mate*[h]

[6]

[a] By devious means we have reached a Giuoco Piano, in which White's early castling will do him no good.

[b] 6 B–K3 is safer.

[c] A more tranquil course was 8 QKt–Q2, Q–Q2; 9 K–R2, O–O–O; 10 P–B3 etc. But the acceptance of the sacrifice is playable!

[d] 10 Kt–Kt4 is probably also good enough.

[e] White's play is not on the same high imaginative level as that of his opponent. 11 P–Q4! gains a priceless tempo by breaking the Bishop's diagonal, so that if, for example, 11 ... P×P; 12 B×Q, P–Q6; 13 B–R4 and wins. 11 ... B×P (12 Q×B!) and 11 ... Kt×QP are likewise inadequate.

[f] Now the combination clicks.

[g] If 15 QKt–Q2, R×R and Black wins easily with two exchanges ahead. The text, however, allows a finish of really poetic splendor.

[h] Derrickson, we are told, "was a youth who possessed the most brilliant and precocious chess talent, and upon whose shoulders it was thought the mantle of Morphy was about to fall. But soon, too soon, grim Death called him from the checkered field on which he had won so many brilliant victories." Emanuel Lasker was very fond of this game, and extolled it because "it demonstrates in beautiful harmony the valuable qualities of a chess player: clear position judgment, bold, far-reaching combination and decisive action at the right moment."

NEGATIVE IMMORTALITY

WE ARE TOLD with equal enthusiasm that man learns from experience, and also that he is a creature of habit. To reconcile these mutually contradictory claims, we must conclude that exceptional men learn from experience, while the rest remain creatures of habit.

A case in point: the great Steinitz quickly saw the fallacy of attack for attack's sake; the mediocre Dufresne contributed over and over again to the making of an immortal game.

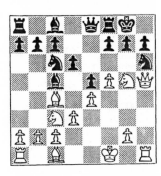

[After 13 ... Q–K1]

KING'S GAMBIT DECLINED

Berlin, 1863

WHITE	BLACK
G. R. Neumann	J. Dufresne
1 P–K4	P–K4
2 P–KB4	B–B4 [a]
3 Kt–KB3	P–Q3
4 B–B4	Kt–KB3
5 Kt–B3	O–O
6 P–Q3	Kt–Kt5? [b]
7 R–B1	Kt×P? [c]
8 R–R1! [d]	Kt–Kt5
9 Q–K2	B–B7ch?
10 K–B1	Kt–QB3
11 P–B5!	B–B4
12 Kt–KKt5!	Kt–R3 [e]

13 Q–R5	Q–K1 [f]*
14 Kt×RP! [g]	K×Kt
15 B×Kt	P–KKt3 [h]
16 Q×Pch!	P×Q
17 B×R mate [i]	

[8]

[a] Very prudent—so far.

[b] Serious neglect of his development. By simply playing 6 ... Kt–B3 he would have had a good game.

[c] Worse yet; he sees a "combination": if 8 Kt×Kt, Q–R5ch etc.

[d] Naturally: having the permanent address of Black's King, Neumann is delighted with the gift of the open King's Rook file.

[e] Black is defenseless (a state to which his futile check for "attack" on move 9 has contributed). If 12 ... Kt–B3; 13 Kt×RP, Kt×Kt; 14 Q–R5 etc.

[f] Or 13 ... Q–B3; 14 Kt×RP!, K×Kt; 15 B–KKt5 winning the Queen!

[g] He plans a superb finish.

[h] Amusing would be 15 ... P–B3; 16 B–B1ch (anywhere else on this diagonal will also do), Q×Q; 17 R×Q mate. White's attack is so brutal that even exchanging Queens leads to mate on the move!

[i] Thus ends the melodrama of The Open File's Revenge! This game must have taught a great deal to ... Steinitz.

GENIUS IN A GARRET

No man but a blockhead," said Dr. Johnson, "ever wrote except for money." If we substitute *played chess* for *wrote*, then, by the terms of this definition, poor Zukertort, who is said to have died of "malnutrition," was indeed a blockhead. Yet the name of Zukertort will always remain an unforgettable synonym for elegant attacking play. When he was still a pupil of Anderssen, he beat his great teacher in the following fashion:

RUY LOPEZ

Berlin, 1865

*[After 10 ... Q–K1]

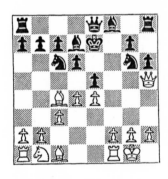

WHITE	BLACK
J. Zukertort	*A. Anderssen*
1 P–K4	P–K4
2 Kt–KB3	Kt–QB3
3 B–Kt5	KKt–K2 [a]
4 P–B3	P–Q3
5 P–Q4	B–Q2
6 O–O	Kt–Kt3
7 Kt–Kt5 [b]	P–KR3? [c]
8 Kt×P!!	K×Kt
9 B–B4ch	K–K2 [d]
10 Q–R5	Q–K1 [e]*

11 Q–Kt5ch!!	P×Q
12 B×P *mate!* [f]	

[*a*] The Cozio Defense, advocated for a time by Steinitz. It constricts Black's game excessively.

[*b*] True to his style, Zukertort loses no time in playing for the attack.

[*c*] The art of defensive play was still a mystery in those days! Steinitz would have played 7 ... Kt–R4—or 7 ... B–K2; 8 Q–R5, B×Kt; 9 B×B, QKt–K2 with a cramped but fairly defensible game.

[*d*] Black caves in. 9 ... P–Q4 would have forced White to work harder to demonstrate the soundness of his sacrifice, the main line being 10 KP×P, Kt–Kt1; 11 Q–R5, B–Q3; 12 B–Q3, Q–B3; 13 P×P, B×P; 14 P–KB4 with a winning attack. Or if 9 ... K–K1; 10 Q–R5, Q–B3; 11 P–KB4 with a powerful game.

[*e*] On 10 ... B–K1 Zukertort planned 11 B–Kt5*ch!*, P×B; 12 Q×P*ch*, K–Q2; 13 Q–B5ch, K–K2; 14 Q–K6 *mate!*

[*f*] The most devastating win ever achieved against a grand-master!

THE AUSTRIAN MORPHY

NATUR," SAID MR. SQUEERS, "is a rum 'un." The greatest of chess history's many ironies was the transformation of Wilhelm Steinitz from a brilliant attacking player into a lifelong partisan of sound positional play.

How Steinitz acquired the nickname of "the Austrian Morphy" in his salad days is convincingly explained by the following game, notable for the bravura and resourcefulness of White's attack.

KIESERITZKY GAMBIT

London, 1866

WHITE	BLACK
W. Steinitz	*Belaiev*

[After 12 ... Q × RP]

	WHITE	BLACK
1	P–K4	P–K4
2	P–KB4	P×P
3	Kt–KB3	P–KKt4
4	P–KR4	P–Kt5
5	Kt–K5	Kt–KB3 [a]
6	B–B4	P–Q4
7	P×P	B–Q3
8	P–Q4	Kt–R4 [b]
9	Kt–QB3	Q–K2 [c]
10	B–Kt5ch?	K–Q1? [d]
11	O–O!	B×Kt
12	P×B	Q×RP [e]*
13	R×P! [f]	Kt×R
14	B×Kt	P–Kt6
15	Q–B3! [g]	R–Kt1
16	P–K6!! [h]	P×P
17	B×P!!	Q–Kt4 [i]
18	Q–B7! [j]	P–K4 [k]
19	Q×Rch!	Q×Q
20	B–R4ch	Resigns [l]

[*a*] An improvement on the older 5 ... P–KR4*?*; 6 B–B4, Kt–KR3; 7 P–Q4 which leaves White with a splendid game.

[*b*] Guarding the gambit Pawn and also anticipating some counterattack in the event that White castles.

[*c*] A fashionable variation in those days was 9 ... Kt–Kt6; 10 B×P, Kt×R "and White has a strong attack." The proof would be interesting.

[*d*] This move and White's last are hard to understand, as 10 ... P–B3 seems feasible and better.

[*e*] Threatening 13 ... P–Kt6. White seems lost!

[*f*] This sacrifice of the exchange is necessary for defensive purposes; at the same time it yields a strong attack.

[*g*] Another versatile move. If now 15 ... Q–R7*ch*; 16 K–B1, Q–R8*ch*; 17 K–K2, Q×R; 18 B–Kt5*ch* leads to mate.

[*h*] Beautiful! Black's Bishop is bottled up, the King's Bishop file pried open.

[*i*] The better part of valor: if 17 ... Q×B; 18 Q–B6 *mate*; or if 17 ... R×B; 18 Q–B8 *mate*.

[*j*] Threatening 19 Q×P *mate* or 19 B×P *mate*.

[*k*] The last gasp. If 18 ... Q×B; 19 Q–B6 *mate*. And if 18 ... Kt–Q2; 19 P×P wins most simply (19 B–KR4 and 19 Kt–K4 also win).

[*l*] Mate next move! Beautiful though this game is, it must have left Steinitz dissatisfied because of the superficial opening play.

CHESS CARNIVAL

THE VIENNESE MASTER HAMPPE took delight in placing his King in the center of the battle, blandly guiding him to a safe haven in due course. This idiosyncrasy taught the great Steinitz to respect the resiliency of seemingly lost positions.

In later years, Steinitz and his disciple Nimzovich became so adept at defensive policy that they often chortled: "My King likes to go for a walk!" It is a viewpoint more to be enjoyed than imitated.

You can sense, in the carefree play that follows, the now legendary spirit of the Vienna of Johann Strauss: there is a gracious blend of abandon and laughter in this extraordinary contest. Those days were the carnival time of chess.

VIENNA GAME

Vienna, 1872

*[After 9 P-QR3]

WHITE	BLACK
L. Hamppe	P. Meitner
1 P–K4	P–K4
2 Kt–QB3	B–B4
3 Kt–R4!?	B×P*ch!?*
4 K×B	Q–R5*ch* [a]
5 K–K3	Q–B5*ch*
6 K–Q3	P–Q4
7 K–B3	Q×KP
8 K–Kt3	Kt–QR3
9 P–QR3*	Q×Kt*ch!!*
10 K×Q	Kt–B4*ch*
11 K–Kt4	P–R4*ch!*
12 K×Kt	Kt–K2 [b]
13 B–Kt5 *ch*	K–Q1
14 B–B6!	P–Kt3*ch!*
15 K–Kt5	Kt×B [c]
16 K×Kt	B–Kt2*ch!!*
17 K–Kt5! [d]	B–R3*ch*
18 K–B6! [e]	B–Kt2*ch!*
	Drawn!!!

[14]

[*a*] Black has lost no time in making the sacrifice which his opponent provoked. The sequel is astounding.

[*b*] Black is a Queen and two pieces down, but he will have no trouble getting a draw! The immediate threat is 13 ... P–Kt3*ch*; 14 K–Kt5, B–Q2 *mate.*

[*c*] Now the threat is 16 ... Kt–Q5*ch*; 17 K–R4, B–Q2 *mate.* Hilarious would be 16 P–Q4, Kt × P*ch*; 17 Q × Kt, B–Q2 *mate!*

[*d*] Not 17 K × B*??*, K–Q2*!!* and mate is unavoidable.

[*e*] If 18 K–R4*??*, B–B5*!* followed by 19 ... P–Kt4 *mate!*

The attentive reader will note that the drawn result of this game (as well·as of those on page. 118 and page 152) contradicts the subtitle of this book. By way of explanation it may be pointed out that these three games are among the most entertaining in this collection. It is also true that in each of these three games, the attack would have succeeded against any but the very finest defense.

THE UNPARDONABLE SIN

SOME ERRORS OF JUDGMENT violate such familiar principles that the lapses are unpardonable when committed by a master. Such a blunder is seen here on Black's eighth move, when he permits the irrevocable breakup of his Kingside. Only ten moves later, he hears his opponent announce a forced mate!

Nowadays, such crude misplays are largely limited to the games of inexperienced players. In justice to Mason, however, it must be emphasized that basic principles were not so well understood in 1878 as they are today.

FRENCH DEFENSE   *[After 16 ... QR–KKt1]*

Paris, 1878

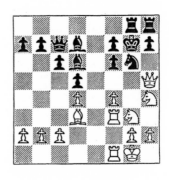

WHITE	BLACK
G. *Mackenzie*	*J. Mason*
1 P–K4	P–K3
2 P–Q4	P–Q4
3 Kt–QB3	Kt–KB3
4 P×P	P×P
5 Kt–B3	B–Q3 [a]
6 B–Q3	O–O
7 O–O	Kt–B3 [b]
8 B–KKt5	Kt–K2?? [c]
9 B×Kt	P×B
10 Kt–KR4 [d]	K–Kt2
11 Q–R5	R–R1
12 P–B4	P–B3 [e]
13 R–B3	Kt–Kt3
14 QR–KB1	Q–B2

15 Kt–K2!	B–Q2
16 Kt–Kt3 [f]	QR–KKt1*
17 Q–R6*ch!!*	

White announced mate in five more moves. [g]

[*a*] The game has transposed into the Exchange Variation, which gives Black an easy game if he plays with reasonable care. 5 ... B–K2, for example, avoids the subsequent pin on the King's Knight.

[*b*] And here the more comfortable course is 7 ... B–KKt5; 8 B–KKt5, P–B3; 9 P–KR3, B×Kt (else 9 ... B–R4; 10 P–KKt4, B–Kt3; 11 Kt–K5 gives Black a hard game); 10 Q×B, QKt–Q2.

[*c*] Permitting a fatal weakness. 8 ... B–K2 was far better, despite the loss of time involved.

[*d*] White's task is obvious: to concentrate his attacking forces against Black's pitiably exposed King. Although this procedure is far from taxing to a player of master strength, Mackenzie deserves praise for the economical way in which he mounts the offensive on the King-side.

[*e*] White was threatening 13 Kt×P.

[*f*] Black has no good moves. If for example 16 ... QR–K1; 17 Kt(3)–B5*ch*, K–Kt1 (not 17 ... K–B1*??*; 18 Q–R6*ch* and mate next move. Or 17 ... B×Kt; 18 Kt×B*ch*, K–Kt1; 19 Kt×B, Q×Kt; 20 P–B5, Kt–K2; 21 R–Kt3*ch* and wins); 18 Kt–R6*ch*, K–B1; 19 P–B5 and wins.
After 16 ... B×P or 16 ... Kt×P, a Knight check at B5 is likewise decisive.

[*g*] A sparkling finish. After 17 ... K×Q (must!) there follows 18 Kt(4)–B5*ch*, B×Kt; 19 Kt×B*ch*, K–R4; 20 P–Kt4*ch*, K×P; 21 R–Kt3*ch*, K–R4; 22 B–K2 *mate!*

BOOK VARIATIONS

IT IS BECOMING INCREASINGLY OBVIOUS that is a few centuries chess will be completely played out. In some openings, such as the Ruy Lopez, Queen's Gambit Declined and Nimzoindian Defense, we now have variations in which the best moves for both players are clearly mapped out for the first 25 moves or so. As the area of such "taken-for-granted" moves widens, chess will become more a test of memory and less a test of ability.

When this stage of chess development arrives, players will look back nostalgically to the good old days when the masters were more or less on their own and had untrammeled play for the imagination. And yet, even in bygone days, memory was a far from negligible factor in opening theory. The point is graphically made in the following game.

SCOTCH GAME

Match, 1888

[After 11 Q-K2]

WHITE	BLACK
E. Delmar	S. Lipschuetz

1	P-K4	P-K4	
2	Kt-KB3	Kt-QB3	
3	P-Q4	P×P	
4	Kt×P	Kt-B3	
5	Kt×Kt	KtP×Kt	
6	B-Q3	P-Q4 [a]	
7	P-K5?	Kt-Kt5	
8	O-O	B-QB4 [b]	13 K-R1 [h]	B×P! [i]
9	P-KR3 [c]	Kt×KP! [d]	14 P×B	Q-B6ch
10	R-K1	Q-B3! [e]	15 K-R2	B-Q3
11	Q-K2 [f]*	O-O! [g]	16 Q×B	Q-B7ch! [j]
12	Q×Kt	Q×Pch	Resigns [k]

[18]

[a] Black always equalizes easily in this opening. Attempts by White to seize a violent initiative recoil on him with redoubled violence. Here White's best course is 7 P×P etc.

[b] But not 8 ... Kt×KP?; 9 R–K1 and White wins a piece.

[c] Still angling for the pin. If instead 9 B–KB4, P–KKt4!; 10 B–Kt3, P–KR4 and White is in trouble.

[d] Involves a brilliant finesse.

[e] Despite its risky appearance, this is much stronger than the apparently obligatory 10 ... P–B3.

[f] A critical situation for Black: the Knight cannot be saved. What to do?

[g] An engagingly simple solution. The loss of the Knight has already been discounted by Lipschuetz.

[h] If 13 K–R2, B–Q3 wins the Queen.

[i] To prevent the threatened mate, White must give up the Queen.

[j] In order to pick up the Rook with check before capturing the Queen.

[k] Steinitz comments: "We learn that the game, as played here, is already forestalled in an analysis of this opening by Professor Berger . . . but Mr. Lipschuetz assures us that he had never seen it."

STEINITZ ATTACKS!

S O MUCH HAS BEEN WRITTEN about Steinitz's superlative defensive skill that we are apt to lose sight of the fact that he was an equally great master of the attack. Nor is there anything paradoxical in this. Steinitz began his career with a natural bent for attacking play, but he soon made the revolutionary discovery that successful attacks must be based on previously acquired advantages. And so he turned to defensive play by sheer force of logic and will power: he had learned from bitter experience that there is a time to attack, and a time to defend. That his view of the matter was by no means one-sided is clear from the following superb game:

FRENCH DEFENSE   *[After 9 ... P–B3]*
Havana, 1888

WHITE	BLACK
W. Steinitz	*C. Golmayo*

	WHITE	BLACK		
1	P–K4	P–K3		
2	P–Q4	P–Q4		
3	Kt–QB3	Kt–KB3		
4	P–K5	KKt–Q2		
5	P–B4	P–QB4		
6	P×P	B×P		
7	Kt–B3	O–O		
8	B–Q3	Kt–QB3? [a]		
9	P–KR4	P–B3 [b]*		
10	Kt–KKt5!!	P×Kt [c]	15	P–KKt4!	R×P ch
11	B×P ch!	K×B [d]	16	K–Q1	B–K6 [h]
12	P×P ch	K–Kt1 [e]	17	B×B	R×B [i]
13	Q–R5	Kt(2)×P [f]	18	Kt–Kt5!!	R–B6 [j]
14	P×Kt	R–B4 [g]	19	P–Kt6	Resigns [k]

[*a*] Too slow. As White obviously plans action on the King-side, Black should have countered promptly with 8 ... P–B3.

[*b*] Now comes a masterly combination.

[*c*] Forced, as both the KRP and KP were attacked.

[*d*] There is more resistance in the interesting alternative 11 ... K–B2; 12 Q–R5*ch*, K–K2; 13 Q×P*ch*, K–K1 (not 13 ... K–B2*?*; 14 B–Kt6*ch*, K–Kt1; 15 Q–R5 etc.); 14 B–Kt6*ch*, R–B2; 15 Q–R5, Q–K2; 16 Kt–Kt5, Kt–Kt3; 17 B×R*ch*, Q×B; 18 Kt–B7*ch* and White wins by material advantage.

[*e*] And not 12 ... K–Kt3*?*; 13 Q–R5*ch*, K–B4; 14 P–Kt4 *mate*—a pretty tableau.

[*f*] On 13 ... Kt–K2 (to meet 14 P–Kt6) Steinitz intended 14 Kt×P*!*, Q–R4*ch* (if 14 ... P×Kt; 15 P–K6 or 14 ... Kt×Kt; 15 P–Kt6); 15 K–Q1, Kt×P; 16 Kt–B6*ch!!*, R×Kt; 17 P×R and White wins *both* Knights!

[*g*] After 14 ... B–B7*ch*; 15 K–Q1, Kt×P; 16 P–Kt6, Kt×P; 17 Q×Kt, Q–B3; 18 Q–R7*ch*, K–B2; 19 R–B1 White has a winning game.

[*h*] Or 16 ... P–Q5; 17 Kt–K4*!* (threatens 18 Kt–B6*ch*), R×Kt; 18 R–B1, Kt–K4; 19 P–Kt6, Kt×P(3); 20 Q×Kt and wins.

[*i*] If now 18 P–Kt6, K–B1; 19 Q–R8*ch*, K–K2; 20 Q×P*ch*, K–Q3. This explains White's next move.

[*j*] To stop a later check by White's Rook. If instead 18 ... Kt–K4; 19 Q–R8*ch* wins Black's Queen.

[*k*] For if 19 ... K–B1; 20 Q–R8*ch*, K–K2; 21 Q×Pch and mate next move. White's attack was a masterpiece of intricate calculation.

QUIET, PLEASE!

I T WAS THAT EXUBERANT PHRASE-MAKER and paradox-monger Dr. Tartakover who once remarked that a Pawn sacrifice requires more skill than does a Queen sacrifice. The reason? Sacrificing the Queen calls for exact calculation of a quick finish. The Pawn sacrifice, on the other hand, involves an intuitive flair possessed as a rule only by the great masters.

On a par with the subtle Pawn sacrifice is the surrender of the exchange followed by a clever series of "quiet" moves. Precisely because of their refinement and lack of flamboyant qualities, such combinations are generally "born to blush unseen."

GIUOCO PIANO
Nuremberg, 1892

[After 12 ... B–Kt5]

WHITE	BLACK
Dr. S.	S.
Tarrasch	Taubenhaus

1	P–K4	P–K4
2	Kt–KB3	Kt–QB3
3	B–B4	Kt–B3
4	P–Q3	B–B4
5	P–B3	P–Q3
6	B–K3	B–Kt3
7	QKt–Q2	B–K3
8	B–QKt5	O–O
9	Q–K2	Kt–K2
10	P–Q4	Kt–Kt3
11	O–O	Kt–R4 [a]
12	P–KKt3! [b]	B–Kt5 [c]*
13	P–KR3!!	B×RP

14	Kt–Kt5!!	B×R [d]
15	Q×Kt	P–KR3
16	Kt×B!	P×Kt
17	B×P [e]	Kt–K2 [f]
18	Kt–K3	P×P [g]
19	Kt–Q5	P–KB3
20	B–QB4!	Resigns [h]

[*a*] Despite the deceptive pianissimo beginning, the crisis has arrived: can Black be allowed to plant a Knight on the powerful outpost KB5? 12 Kt×P?? is no help, for then 12 ... Kt(4)–B5 wins a piece. And 12 P–KKt3 is much too risky because of 12 ... B–Kt5 threatening such moves as ... P–KB4 and ... Q–B3 with a tremendous attack.

[*b*] Nevertheless!

[*c*] Of course. White's predicament is now very serious.

[*d*] Black cannot believe his eyes. Why this generosity?!

[*e*] White has given up the exchange, but there is a price tag on it. His Queen and two Bishops are strongly entrenched, and his Knight will soon join the attack. None of Black's pieces is effective, and his King is without a friend in the world.

[*f*] The reader is entreated to study this instructive variation: 17 ... Q–B1 (not 17 ... P–KB3??; 18 B–B4*ch* etc.); 18 B–QB4! (threatens 19 Q×Kt), P–B3 (if 18 ... Kt–R1 the entry of White's Knight decides quickly); 19 Kt–K3 (not 19 Q×Kt, P–Q4), P×P; 20 Kt–Kt4 (threatens Kt–B6*ch* or Kt–R6*ch*), P–Q4; 21 K–Kt2!, P×B; 22 R–R1 (*et tu, Brute?*), P–B3 (or 22 ... R–K1; 23 Q–R7*ch*, K–B1; 24 Q–R8*ch*! and mate next move); 23 Kt–R6*ch*, K–R2; 24 Kt–B5*ch*, K–Kt1; 25 Kt–Q6 and wins!

[*g*] On 18 ... P–QB3 he also gets short shrift: 19 B–QB4, Q–Q2; 20 Kt–Kt4, P–Q4; 21 Kt–B6*ch*!, P×Kt; 22 B×BP, Kt–Kt3; 23 Q–R6 and mate next move.

[*h*] He's had enough. If 20 ... Kt×Kt (or 20 ... R–B2; 21 Kt×P*ch*! with a quick mate); 21 B×Kt*ch* and mate in two.

CASTLING INTO IT

BLACKBURNE WAS A GREAT MASTER of the attack. On the Continent they punned on his name with the mordant nickname "the Black Death." In some of his games, he achieved the decision so rapidly that it almost seemed as if occult forces were at work: his opponent seemed to play "just those moves" which were needed for a delightful splash of fireworks. Perhaps it was "black magic"; perhaps, to use Emanuel Lasker's term, "white magic." Whatever the cause, the result was usually a rewarding brilliancy.

CENTER GAME
Hastings, 1894

WHITE	BLACK
	J. H.
Allies	*Blackburne*
1 P–K4	P–K4
2 P–Q4	P×P
3 Q×P	Kt–QB3
4 Q–K3	P–KKt3 [*a*]
5 B–Q2	B–Kt2
6 Kt–QB3 [*b*]	KKt–K2 [*c*]
7 O–O–O	O–O
8 P–B4? [*d*]	P–Q4! [*e*]
9 P×P	Kt–Kt5!
10 B–B4	B–B4 [*f*]
11 B–Kt3	KKt×P
12 Kt×Kt	Kt×Kt
13 Q–KB3	Q–B3! [*g*]

[After 15 ... Q–R3!!]

14 P–B3	Kt–Kt5! [*h*]
15 B–B4	Q–R3!! [*i*]*
16 P–Kt4 [*j*]	Q×P!! [*k*]
17 B–K3	B×BP!!
	Resigns [*l*]

[*a*] Anticipating that White will castle Queen-side, Black-burne trains his Bishop on that sector.

[*b*] It would have been wiser to neutralize the hostile Bishop with 6 B–B3.

[*c*] 6 ... Kt–KB3 would block the Bishop's diagonal.

[*d*] With the players castled on opposite wings, their moves must be sharp and accurate. The text is slow: 8 Kt–Q5 (intending 9 B–B3) would be far better.

[*e*] Snatching the initiative, as ... P–Q5 is threatened.

[*f*] Black develops more rapidly—and with threats.

[*g*] No defensive moves! The gain of time (mate is menaced) gives Black a lasting initiative. The lasting initiative lasts just four moves—enough to force White's surrender!

[*h*] The Knight is immune from capture, and the threat is ... Kt–Q6*ch* followed by a discovery winning the White Queen.

[*i*] Superb play. If 15 B×Q, Kt×P *mate!*

[*j*] So that if 16 ... Q×B; 17 P×B and White can hold out for a while.

[*k*] Blackburne is pitiless. If now 17 B×Q, Kt×B *mate*; if 17 P×B, Q–R8 *mate*.

[*l*] He is threatened with three mates on the move, and if 18 P×KB, a fourth mate turns up: 18 ... Q–B7 *mate*.

DR. LIVINGSTONE, I PRESUME?

I N CHESS THERE IS OFTEN a nerve-rending clash between the desire for adventure and a prudent preference for being safe rather than sorry. The urge to play exotic openings, with their avoidance of the all-too-familiar and banal, is one which every explorer would readily recognize and appreciate. But the leap into uncharted regions has its inevitable dangers as well as illusory attractions.

As early as the eighth move, poor Fleissig must have wished that he had remained in the prosaic haven of the Giuoco Piano or Ruy Lopez!

ORANGOUTANG
OPENING

Vienna, 1895

WHITE	BLACK
B. Fleissig	*C. Schlechter*
1 P–QKt4	P–K3
2 B–Kt2	Kt–KB3
3 P–QR3	P–B4
4 P–Kt5	P–Q4 [*a*]
5 P–Q4?	Q–R4*ch!* [*b*]
6 Kt–B3	Kt–K5
7 Q–Q3	P×P
8 Q×P	B–B4!
9 Q×KtP	B×P*ch*
10 K–Q1*	P–Q5!! [*c*]
11 Q×R*ch*	K–K2!
12 Q×B [*d*]	P×Kt
13 B–B1 [*e*]	Kt–Q2!!

[After 10 K–Q1]

14 Q×R [*f*]	Q×KtP [*g*]
15 B–B4	Q–Q4*ch*
16 K–B1	B–K6*ch!!* [*h*]
17 B×B	Kt–B7!!
	Resigns [*i*]

[a] Black has proceeded with sound development, while his opponent has indulged in mere eccentricity. The following move, however, is a clear mistake.

[b] In order to guard the exposed QKtP, Fleissig must subject himself to a disastrous pin.

[c] Beginning one of the grand combinations of chess history. White's Knight cannot move (11 Kt × Kt?, Q–K8 *mate*). Hence he solaces his misfortunes with a Rook or two.

[d] "Appetite grows with eating." The fact is, though, that even against more abstemious moves, such as 12 Kt–B3, Black would simply play . . . P × Kt with a winning attack.

[e] Another way is 13 B × P, Kt × B*ch*; 14 K–Q2, Kt–K5*ch*; 15 K–Q3, Q–Q7*ch*; 16 K × Kt, Q–K6 *mate*.

[f] Black's last move was only the prelude to more sacrifices. The point is that White's Queen cannot participate in the defense: 14 Q–B4, R–Q1; 15 Q–Kt4*ch* (if 15 Q × Kt, Kt–B4*ch*; 16 Q–Q3, Kt × Q; 17 KP × Kt Black wins without trouble), Kt–B4*ch*; 16 B–Q2, R × B*ch*; 17 K–B1, and now Cherney gives 17 . . . R–Q8*ch!!*; 18 K × R, Q–Q1*ch*; 19 K–B1, Q–Q7*ch*; 20 K–Kt1, Q–Q8*ch*; 21 K–Kt2, Q × P*ch*; 22 Q–Kt2, Q × Q *mate*.
And if 14 Q × KtP, R–Q1 and the threat of 15 . . . Kt(5)–B4 followed by a discovery with the other Knight is decisive.

[g] Now there is no defense to the coming . . . Q–Q4*ch*. Try, for example, 15 Kt–B3, Q–Q4*ch*; 16 B–Q2, P × B; 17 P–B4, Kt–B6*ch*; 18 K–B2, P–Q8(Q)*ch* with mate in the offing.

[h] An exquisite move. Obviously White must capture.

[i] For if 18 B × Kt, Q–Q7*ch*; 19 K–Kt1, Q–Q8*ch*; 20 K–R2, Q × P *mate*. A glorious finish!

[27]

DON QUIXOTE OF THE
CHESSBOARD

JANOWSKI FRITTERED AWAY A LIFETIME of chessplaying in his efforts to imitate the brilliant chess of his youth. For the thrills which he missed in his later games, he substituted the artificial excitement of the roulette wheel. Chess devotees of a subsequent generation have had to accept on trust the glamorous tales of his combinative artistry; sometimes it was a grudging acceptance, for the deeds of current heroes are more impressive than the tattered sagas of faraway tournaments. But the following charming miniature shows us how Janowski played at his inimitably dashing best:

QUEEN'S GAMBIT

Nuremberg, 1896

WHITE	BLACK
D. Janowski	*E. Schallopp*
1 P–Q4	P–Q4
2 P–QB4	P×P
3 Kt–KB3	P–QB4
4 P–K3	P×P
5 P×P	B–Kt5? [a]
6 B×P	P–K3 [b]
7 Q–R4ch!	Kt–B3 [c]
8 Kt–K5	Q×P [d]
9 Kt×Kt	Q–K5ch
10 B–K3	P×Kt
11 Kt–B3	Q×P [e]
12 B–Q5!!*	P×B
13 Q×Pch	K–Q1 [f]

[After 12 B–Q5!!]

14 Q×Rch	K–Q2
15 Q–Kt7ch	K–K3
16 Q–B6ch	B–Q3
17 B–B4!	Resigns [g]

[28]

[*a*] As a disciple of the immortal Anderssen, Schallopp inherited two qualities: he was fond of mettlesome play, and he allowed the Queen's Pawn openings to remain a book sealed with seven seals. No quicker recipe for disaster could be evolved than the unfortunate combination of these qualities.

The rash opening up of the game (3 ... P–QB4) followed by the weakening of the Queen-side (5 ... B–Kt5?) only plays into Janowski's hands.

[*b*] White threatened 7 B × P*ch*.

[*c*] Inadequate, but what else has he? If 7 ... Kt–Q2; 8 Kt–K5, Kt–B3; 9 B–KKt5!, B–KB4; 10 Kt × Kt, Q × Kt; 11 B–Kt5 winning the Queen!

[*d*] He means to bluster it out with brazen counterattack.

[*e*] Precariously clinging to the ailing QBP. But Janowski brutally elbows him aside.

[*f*] Or 13 ... K–K2; 14 Kt × P*ch*, K–Q1; 15 Q × R*ch* and Black can resign.

[*g*] For if 17 ... Q × R*ch*; 18 K–Q2, Q × R; 19 Q × B*ch* and mate in two more moves. A saucy little game.

TO BE OR NOT TO BE . . .

CRUSTY OLD WILHELM STEINITZ lived in an era when attacking play was all the rage. Yet he had a fanatical faith in the efficacy of defense. Right up to the very brink of old age, he successfully maintained his theories against a chess world which despised them but could not defeat them. As he grew older, his stubborn attitude cost him many an irretrievable point; but he never flinched from subjecting himself to tasks which would have terrified lesser—or lazier—men.

In this game we witness a tragic collapse of his defensive powers; yet we cannot help admiring him for the sturdy courage of his convictions.

CENTER GAME
Nuremberg, 1896

[After 17 B–K4]

	WHITE	BLACK
	S. *Winawer*	W. *Steinitz*
1	P–K4	P–K4
2	P–Q4	P×P
3	Q×P [a]	Kt–QB3
4	Q–K3	Kt–B3 [b]
5	Kt–QB3	B–Kt5
6	B–Q2	O–O
7	O–O–O	R–K1
8	B–QB4!?	B×Kt [c]
9	B×B	Kt×P [d]
10	Q–B4	Kt–B3
11	Kt–B3	P–Q3
12	Kt–Kt5	B–K3
13	B–Q3	P–KR3
14	P–KR4! [e]	Kt–Q4 [f]
15	B–R7ch! [g]	K–R1 [h]
16	R×Kt!	B×R
17	B–K4 [i]*	P–B3? [j]
18	B×B	BP×Kt
19	P×P	Kt–K4 [k]
20	P–Kt6!	Resigns [l]

[30]

[*a*] The loss of time this entails has put the opening in the same class with the ichthyosaurus.

[*b*] For 4 ... P–KKt3 see Allies–Blackburne, page 24.

[*c*] Steinitz goes after the proffered Pawn, although he knows that he will have a difficult time.

[*d*] But not 9 ... R×P?; 10 B×Kt and wins!

[*e*] Quite right: his material inferiority forbids retreat. Yet Black must play with great care, in view of the menacing way that the hostile pieces glare at his King.

[*f*] After 14 ... P×Kt?; 15 P×P Black would be lost; take this brilliant possibility: 15 ... Kt–Q4; 16 R–R8*ch!*, K×R; 17 Q–R4*ch*, K–Kt1; 18 B×P*!*, K×B; 19 Q–R6*ch*, K–Kt1; 20 R–R1 and mate is unavoidable.

[*g*] This ingenious move forces Black's reply, for if 15 ... K–B1; 16 Kt×B*ch*, R×Kt; 17 R×Kt wins.

[*h*] Black seems to be in the clear, as he is about to remove White's mighty Queen's Bishop. Winawer seizes his only chance.

[*i*] Threatens 18 Kt×P*ch!*, B×Kt; 19 Q×P*ch* and mate next move!

[*j*] Fatigue. He should have broken the attack with 17 ... R×B*!*; 18 Kt×R, Kt–K4; 19 Kt×P*!*, Q×Kt*!* (if 19 ... P×Kt; 20 R–Q1 regains the piece advantageously); 20 B×Kt, Q–QB3; 21 R–Q1, B–K5 (not 21 ... B×RP?; 22 R–Q6*!*) with equality.

[*k*] 20 R×P *mate* was threatened. (19 ... Q×P?? cannot be played!)

[*l*] He has no defense against the coming 21 R×P*ch!* The operation was a great success, but the patient died. Steinitz appraised the attack correctly, but the practical difficulties proved too great.

ACHILLES HEEL

The ATTRACTION OF THE KING'S GAMBIT lies in the fact that it concentrates White's attack against Black's KB2—the weakest point in Black's position during the early part of the game. This target is particularly vulnerable to combined attack by a White Bishop at QB4, a White Knight at K5 or KKt5, a White Rook at KB1 and the White Queen at KR5.

Tchigorin, who was famous for his mastery of all forms of the King's Gambit, produced many a charming brilliancy by his practiced utilization of these factors. His combination here, while not profound, is pleasantly neat and crisp.

BISHOP'S GAMBIT

London, 1899

[After 13 ... Q–Kt3]

	WHITE	BLACK
	M. Tchigorin	C. Schlechter
1	P–K4	P–K4
2	P–KB4	P×P
3	B–B4	Kt–KB3
4	Kt–QB3	Kt–B3 [a]
5	Kt–B3	B–Kt5
6	O–O	O–O [b]
7	P–K5 [c]	Kt–Kt5
8	P–Q4	P–Q3
9	P–KR3	Kt–K6
10	B×Kt	P×B
11	Kt–Q5	B–R4
12	P×P	Q×P? [d]
13	Kt–Kt5!	Q–Kt3 [e]*

14	Kt×BP!	R×Kt [f]
15	Kt–K7ch	Kt×Kt
16	B×Rch	Q×B
17	R×Q	Resigns [g]

[32]

[*a*] In the later game Silverman–Eliskases (page 122), Black played 4 ... P–B3, with a view to blocking the Bishop's diagonal. There is, however, a certain similarity in the later play of both games. In each case, the weak point KB7 is taken by storm!

[*b*] ... P–Q3 first is safer, helping to maintain Black's Knight at KB3.

[*c*] In reply to this advance, Steinitz once made a successful defense against Charousek with 7 ... Kt–K1; 8 Kt–Q5, B–R4; 9 P–Q4, P–Q3. Black's position, however, could afford pleasure to no one but a Steinitz!

[*d*] Fatal: he should have played 12 ... P × P (unattractive as it looks) to prevent White's next move.

[*e*] There is no balm in Gilead, for if instead 13 ... B–K3; 14 Q–R5, P–KR3; 15 Kt–K4!, Q–Q1; 16 Kt(Q5)–B6*ch!*, P × Kt (if 16 ... K–R1; 17 P–Q5 wins); 17 Q × P with a quick win.

[*f*] Schlechter is succumbing to the classic form of attack in the King's Gambit.

[*g*] For if 17 ... K × R; 18 Q–R5*ch* picks up Black's Bishop at QR4.

"A PARADOX, A PARADOX . . ."

PAUL MORPHY hit on a literally epoch-making contribution to chess theory when he discovered the value and importance of efficient development. Specializing in gambit lines in his skittle and blindfold play, he realized almost as a matter of course that it was vital to bring out his pieces quickly and effectively.

Yet the masters who came after Morphy were often sleazy in their treatment of the opening. Here, for example, we see Tchigorin, generally considered the greatest player and theoretician of the Romantic school, getting a lost game on the sixth move! Truly "a paradox, a paradox, a most ingenious paradox"; but the punishment, classic and swift, fits the crime.

VIENNA GAME
Moscow, 1899

[After 12 P-QR3]

WHITE	BLACK
M. Tchigorin	*Allies*

1	P-K4	P-K4	
2	Kt-QB3	Kt-KB3	
3	P-B4	P-Q4	
4	P-Q3? [a]	KP×P! [b]	
5	B×P	B-QKt5! [c]	
6	P-K5? [d]	P-Q5! [e]	
7	P×Kt	P×Kt	
8	Q-K2ch? [f]	B-K3	
9	P-QKt3	P×P	15 B-K3 B×Kt
10	Q-K4	Kt-B3	16 Q×B [j] Kt-Q5
11	Kt-B3	Q-Q2	17 Q-B2 R×Bch! [k]
12	P-QR3 [g]*	O-O-O! [h]	18 K-Q1 Q-Kt5ch
13	P×B	B-Q4	19 K-B1 Q-B5!!
14	Q-K2	QR-K1 [i]	*Resigns [l]*

[34]

[*a*] Inferior to the standard continuation 4 BP × P.

[*b*] Rarely played, but best. If now 5 P–K5, P–Q5! gives Black the initiative.

[*c*] A very difficult move to meet satisfactorily.

[*d*] 6 P × P, Kt × P; 7 B–Q2, B × Kt; 8 P × B, O–O; 9 Kt–B3, R–K1*ch*; 10 B–K2, Q–K2! is unfavourable for White; the text continuation is even worse!

[*e*] Now Black is assured of the better game no matter how White plays.

[*f*] From worse to worst! How is the King's Bishop to be developed?!

[*g*] 12 O–O–O is too dangerous; and if 12 B–K2, O–O–O; 13 O–O Black gets a magnificent game with 13 ... QR–K1 or 13 ... B–Q4.

[*h*] The sacrifice of the Bishop is a typical nineteenth century flourish: the Allies are beating Tchigorin with his own weapons! Simply 12 ... B–B4 would leave Black with a splendid position, but it must be admitted that his combination is beautifully calculated.
Tchigorin decides to take the Bishop; "a dying man can eat everything."

[*i*] The point of the sacrifice: the play on the open King's file regains the piece in short order.

[*j*] If 16 P × B, Kt–Q5; 17 Q–B2 (or 17 B × Kt, R × Q*ch* with an easy win) and Black wins with 17 ... R × B*ch*!

[*k*] The second point: if 18 Q × R, Kt × P*ch* forks the Queen.

[*l*] For if 20 Q × Q, R–K8 *mate*. Masterly play by the Allies (S. Levitzky and V. Nenarokov).

SANS VOIR

THE ABILITY TO PLAY CHESS without sight of board or men has always been the master's most glamorous attribute. When, in the waning years of the eighteenth century, Philidor succeeded in playing *two* games blindfold, his contemporaries looked on in awe. As the years went by, the number of games increased steadily until, on January 27, 1947, Naidorf played *45* games simultaneously at Sao Paulo!

Harry Nelson Pillsbury, the brilliant American master who died at a tragically early age, was one of the most important figures in the development of blindfold chess.

HAMPPE-ALLGAIER GAMBIT
New York, 1900

[After 15 ... K × P]

WHITE	BLACK
H. N.	*C. S.*
Pillsbury	*Howell*
1 P–K4	P–K4
2 Kt–QB3	Kt–QB3
3 P–B4	P × P
4 Kt–B3	P–KKt4
5 P–KR4	P–Kt5
6 Kt–KKt5	P–KR3
7 Kt × P	K × Kt
8 P–Q4	P–Q4 [a]
9 B × P	B–Kt2
10 B–K3	B–B3? [b]
11 P–KKt3	P × P [c]
12 B–B4ch	K–Kt2
13 O–O	B × QP? [d]

14 R–B7ch	K–Kt3
15 P–R5ch! [e]	K × P*
16 R–Kt7!!!	Kt–K4 [f]
17 K–Kt2! [g]	Kt–Kt3
18 Q–R1ch	Kt–R5ch
19 Q × Ktch	Q × Q
20 B–B7 *mate* [h]	

[a] White has adopted a well-known sacrificial line, giving up a piece in return for superior development and a lasting attack. Black has advanced his QP in the hope that White will capture it and thus block an important line of offense.

[b] Serious loss of time. Better 10 ... Kt–B3 (development!).

[c] Else, after 11 B–K2 and 12 O–O, there will be a nasty threat of P–K5.

[d] Black's game was already somewhat compromised, and 13 ... Kt–R4 was essential to drive White's Bishop away from QB4. The text looks good, but it allows the blindfold player to bring off an enchanting finish.

[e] The key to a combination in the grand manner!

[f] White's last move was incredible for blindfold play! If 16 ... B × R; 17 B–B7 *mate* (magnificent!) or if 16 ... B × B*ch*; 17 K–Kt2 and Black cannot meet both mate threats! Black has therefore played his Knight to K4, preventing B–B7 *mate* and attacking the terrible Bishop. How bitterly Black regrets his 13th move!

[g] A new mating specter appears!

[h] Pure genius! The game is beyond all praise for the imaginative splendor with which it has been conducted by the blindfold player.

A VALUABLE HINT

IF YOU ARE INTERESTED in becoming a good attacking player, note how often the success of an offensive depends on the circumstance that the defender's Queen has been developed prematurely and is picking daisies far from the scene of action. The absence of this powerful piece is of course a severe handicap in the effort to make a successful defense. In the following game, Black's particularly flagrant violation of this elementary defensive rule leads to a finish which is as pretty as it is drastic.

SICILIAN DEFENSE
Brunn, 1905

[After 6 ... Q–B3?]

WHITE	BLACK
J. Brach	*F. Dvorak*
1 P–K4	P–QB4
2 Kt–KB3	P–K3
3 Kt–B3	P–QR3
4 P–Q4	P×P
5 Kt×P	B–B4? [a]
6 B–K3 [b]	Q–B3? [c]*
7 Kt×P!!	B×B
8 Kt–B7ch	K–B1 [d]
9 P×B	R–R2
10 B–B4 [e]	Kt–R3
11 KR–B1	Q–R5ch [f]

12 P–Kt3	Q×RP [g]
13 Q–Q6ch	K–Kt1
14 Kt–K6!!	Resigns [h]

[38]

[a] This old-fashioned move, whose weakness was well-known even in Morphy's day, is the first step to perdition. The subsequent disappearance of the Bishop leaves the vulnerable black squares an easy prey to White's marauding forces. 5 ... P–Q3, followed by 6 ... Kt–KB3, is far better.

[b] Threatening 7 Kt × P!

[c] This anti-positional development of the Queen is easily refuted. The more conservative 6 ... Q–B2 was preferable.

[d] Now Black comprehends the strength of the stinging surprise 7 Kt × P!! If 8 ... K–Q1; 9 P × B, K × Kt??; 10 Kt–Q5ch forking the Queen.

[e] Threatens 11 KR–B1.

[f] Black would doubtless like to keep the Queen nearer home—but how?! If 11 ... Q–Q1?? the forking check 12 Kt–K6ch wins the Queen. If 11 ... Q–Kt3; 12 Kt–K6ch! still wins. On 11 ... Q–K2; 12 Q–Q4 is decisive.

[g] Might as well.

[h] He has no moves. If 14 ... BP × Kt; 15 Q or R–B8 mate. If 14 ... QP × Kt; 15 Q–Q8 mate.

N.N. ET AL.

WE ALL OWE A VOTE OF THANKS for many hours of enjoyment of beautiful chess to our humble friends *N.N.*, *Amateur*, and their quaintly named colleague *A. N. Other*. Handsomely bearing out Milton's observation that "They also serve who only stand and wait," they allow themselves to be used as the raw material for many a charming game.

VIENNA GAME   **[After 13 P–KR3]*

Vienna, 1905

WHITE	BLACK
Amateur	*L. Loewy*
1 P–K4	P–K4
2 Kt–QB3	Kt–KB3
3 P–B4	P–Q4
4 BP×P	Kt×P
5 Kt–B3	Kt–QB3
6 B–Q3? [a]	P–KB4
7 P×P e.p.	Kt×BP
8 O–O	B–B4 ch [b]
9 K–R1	O–O
10 B–Kt5 [c]	Kt–KKt5! [d]
11 B×Kt [e]	P×B
12 P–Q4 [f]	B–Q3 [g]
13 P–KR3 [h]*	B–R3!!

14 P×Kt	B×R
15 Q×B	R×Kt!! [i]
16 Q–K1 [j]	Q–R5ch!!
17 Q×Q	R–B8 *mate*

[*a*] In openings of a predominantly tactical character, such tampering with the rules of common-sense development is often lethal in its consequences. The blocking of the Queen's Bishop's development ultimately costs White the game.

[*b*] This aggressive development is possible because the White QP, being blocked, cannot interpose.

[*c*] Gracefully acknowledging his blunder: he intends P–Q4.

[*d*] A sly rejoinder: he threatens 11 ... Kt–B7*ch*, and 11 P–Q4 can be answered by 11 ... Kt×QP*!*

[*e*] One thing leads to another: in order to force P–Q4, he gives Black's Queen's Bishop a magnificent diagonal.

[*f*] At last he attains his heart's desire, only to drive the Bishop to an equally good diagonal. As Epictetus puts it: "You will find it true that the things that are eagerly followed and admired are of no use to them that have gained them; while they that have not gained them imagine that if they are acquired, everything will come along with them."

[*g*] With a strong threat of 13 ... B–R3.

[*h*] 13 B–Kt5 was more logical; but then 13 ... Q–K1; 14 P–KR3, Q–R4 gives Black a powerful attack.

[*i*] Far more effective than 15 ... Q–R5*ch* (but let's keep that move in reserve!).

[*j*] If 16 Q×R (16 P×R, Q–R5*ch* leads to mate), Q–R5*ch*; 17 K–Kt1 (if 17 Q–R3, Q–K8 *mate*—alas, that undeveloped Queen's Bishop!), Q–K8*ch*; 18 Q–B1, B–R7*ch* wins.

BLUNDER OR BRILLIANCY?!

THERE ARE SOME COMBINATIONS whose objectives are concealed so craftily that you feel certain a blunder has been committed. In such cases, the best course is to take Tarrasch's advice ("sit on your hands!") and subject the position to the most searching scrutiny. If you cannot find a conclusive line of play, look for an *idea* that may offer a clue to your opponent's plans.

In the following game, there is such a clue: the possibility of R–Q8 *mate* turns up in several variations after the Queen sacrifice. This should have given away White's fiendishly ingenious scheme.

DANISH GAMBIT
New York, 1908?

[After 11 ... P–Q4?]

WHITE	BLACK
S.	H. M.
Rubinstein	Phillips
1 P–K4	P–K4
2 P–Q4	P×P
3 P–QB3	P×P
4 B–QB4	P–Q3 [a]
5 Q–Kt3	Q–B3 [b]
6 Kt×P	P–B3
7 Kt–B3	Kt–Q2 [c]
8 B–KKt5	Q–Kt3
9 P–KR4	P–KR4
10 O–O–O	Kt–B4
11 Q–Kt4!!!	P–Q4? [d]*
12 B×P!	Kt–Q6ch [e]
13 R×Kt	B×Q

14 B×KBPch!!	K×B [f]
15 Kt–K5ch	K–K3 [g]
16 Kt×Q	R–R2
17 P–B4	Kt–B3
18 P–B5ch	K–B2
19 R–Q8	P–Kt4 [h]
20 KR–Q1!	Resigns [i]

[a] A cramped but solid defense. For the best line of play see Denker–Gonzalez, page 144.

[b] The Queen is too exposed to attack here. Preferable is 5 ... Q–K2; 6 Kt×P, P–QB3 etc.

[c] 7 ... P–KR3 would have prevented White's next move.

[d] Menacing the Bishop in addition to the threat of ... Kt–Q6*ch*. However, White's last move looks so unnatural that Black should have been on his guard. Yet, while it is all very well to preach general principles, who can blame Black for failing to fathom the coming combination?!

[e] If 12 ... P×B; 13 Kt×P*!*, Kt–Q6*ch* (or 13 ... Kt–QR3; 14 Kt–B7*ch!*, Kt×Kt; 15 R–Q8 *mate*); 14 R×Kt, B×Q; 15 Kt–B7 *mate!*

[f] Now everything becomes painfully clear: if 14 ... Q×B; 15 R–Q8 *mate!*

[g] If 15 ... K–B1; 16 Kt×Q*ch*, K–B2; 17 Kt×R*ch* —and the Knight escapes!

[h] If 19 ... B×P; 20 Kt–K5*ch!* coming out a Rook ahead. After the text, White can win with 20 Kt–K5*ch*, but he chooses an even sharper method.

[i] For if 20 ... B–Kt2; 21 Kt–K5*ch*, K–K2; 22 R(1)–Q7 *mate!* A condensed primer on tactics.

4—(G.370)

THE LAST STRAW

OF MANY A DESPERATELY CRAMPED POSITION it may still be said that while there's life there's hope. As long as the avenues of approach are fairly well blockaded, some semblance of defense is always possible. It is when the lines are opened up that resistance crumbles and brilliant sacrifices become feasible. In the following game, Gunsberg's badly reasoned 16 ... B × Kt? brings on the catastrophe in a most instructive manner.

QUEEN'S GAMBIT
DECLINED

British Championship, 1908

WHITE	BLACK
W. Palmer	*I. Gunsberg*

[After 17 ... P × P]

1 P–Q4	P–Q4
2 P–QB4	P–K3
3 Kt–QB3	B–K2
4 Kt–B3	P–QB3 [a]
5 P–K4	P × KP
6 Kt × P	Kt–B3
7 B–Q3	QKt–Q2
8 O–O	Kt × Kt
9 B × Kt	Kt–B3
10 B–B2	O–O
11 Q–Q3	P–KKt3 [b]
12 B–R6	R–K1
13 Kt–K5	Kt–Q2

14 P–B4	P–QB4 [c]
15 P–Q5!	B–B3 [d]
16 QR–K1	B × Kt? [e]
17 P × B	P × P [f]*
18 R × P!! [g]	Kt × P [h]
19 R–Kt7ch	K–R1
20 R × Kt!	Resigns [i]

[*a*] Black's wheezing play encourages his opponent to proceed energetically.

[*b*] White was threatening to force this weakness by means of B–Kt5. It is already pathetically obvious that Black must dance to White's tune.

[*c*] Trying to free himself, he only plunges deeper into trouble.

[*d*] If 15 ... P×P; 16 Kt×BP*!*, K×Kt; 17 Q×QP*ch*, K–B3; 18 P–B5*!* and wins.

[*e*] Bulldog hanging on with 16 ... Kt–B1 was all that was left. The text opens the KB file, with disastrous consequences.

[*f*] Allowing a neat finish; but with the KB file open, the end is only a matter of time.

[*g*] At once utilizing the open file.

[*h*] If 18 ... K×R; 19 Q×QP*ch*, R–K3; 20 R–B1*ch*, K–K2; 21 B–Kt5*ch* etc.

[*i*] "This is so sudden!" The point is that if 20 ... R×R; 21 R×P*ch!* leads to mate!

TO THE VICTOR

I N THIS GAME between two very enterprising players, there
is a world of difference between the two kinds of enter-
prise! One master takes a risk based on bluff, while his
opponent seasons his daring with solid variations.

Many of the games in the thirty-year duel between Spielmann
and Tartakover had this sharply contrasted character. In view
of their marked combinative talents, it is queer that the spoils
of victory generally went to the player who relied on sober
positional principles; sprightly attacking play usually missed
the target. In this game, Tartakover gives a witty lecture on
the power of the Bishops.

RUY LOPEZ
Munich, 1909

*[After 11 B × BP]

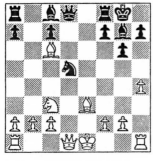

WHITE	BLACK
R. Spielmann	S. Tartakover

1	P–K4	P–K4
2	Kt–KB3	Kt–QB3
3	B–Kt5	KKt–K2 [a]
4	Kt–B3	P–KKt3?
5	P–Q4!	P × P
6	Kt × P? [b]	B–Kt2
7	B–K3	O–O
8	P–KR4??	P–Q4!!
9	P × P	Kt × P! [c]
10	Kt(4) × Kt	P × Kt
11	B × BP*	Kt × B! [d]
12	P × Kt	R–Kt1
13	Q × Q [e]	R × Q

14	O–O [f]	R × P
15	Kt–Q5	B–QR3
16	QR–Q1 [g]	R–Q3! [h]
17	R–B2 [i]	K–B1
18	B–R4	P–QB3!
	Resigns [j]	

[46]

[*a*] The inferior Cozio Defense. See also Zukertort–Anderssen, page 10.

[*b*] Amazingly thoughtless for such a brilliant player as Spielmann. 6 Kt–Q5! (incidentally threatening mate) gives White much the better game: 6 ... B–Kt2 (or 6 ... Kt×Kt; 7 P×Kt, Kt–K2; 8 Q×P etc.); 7 B–Kt5! and White's game plays itself.

[*c*] Black has correctly met an unsound wing attack with a strong counter in the center. If now 10 B×Kt, Kt× Kt!; 11 P×Kt, P×B Black has an ideal two-Bishop situation.

[*d*] And if now 12 Q×Q, Kt×BP*ch!* with much the better game in all variations.

[*e*] Scurrying for safety. The abject 13 Q–B1 is hopeless: 13 ... B×Kt*ch*; 14 P×B, Q–B3; 15 B–B3, Q×BP*ch*; 16 K–B2, R–Kt7; 17 B–Q1, R–Q1 etc.

[*f*] The strongest rejoinder to 14 Kt–Q1 is 14 ... B–QR3!; 15 QR–Kt1, R–Kt3; 16 B–B3, R(3)–Q3 with decisive pressure.

[*g*] 16 KR–Q1, K–B1 offers no hope; Black's Bishops are too strong, White's Pawns too weak. A possibility: 17 Kt×P?, R–B1!; 18 Kt×B, R×B or 18 R–Q7, R–Kt3 winning a piece in either event!

[*h*] After 16 ... B×R; 17 Kt–K7*ch*, K–B1; 18 R×R*ch*, K×Kt; 19 R–Q7*ch* and 20 K×B White has a game of sorts.

[*i*] The alternatives were 17 Kt–K7*ch*, K–B1; 18 R×R, P×R winning the exchange, or 17 KR–K1, B–B6!; 18 Kt×B, R×B and White can resign.

[*j*] For if 19 Kt–B3, B×Kt!; 20 R×R, R–Kt8*ch*; 21 K–R2, B–K4*ch* confiscating the Rook. What Bishops!

[47]

TACTICS BEFORE STRATEGY

EDWARD LASKER ENJOYS THE DISTINCTION of having written one of the first large-scale works dealing with the most important concepts of positional chess. This book (*Chess Strategy*) was a trail-blazer in its day, and unquestionably made a vital contribution to the improvement of playing strength throughout the chess world.

Since the publication of Lasker's classic, there has been such a spate of books stressing strategical play that the emphasis in chess pedagogy has become lop-sided. The importance of tactics is again gaining recognition. It is therefore interesting to have an example of Lasker's gifts as a tactician in the following game played against his brother.

GIUOCO PIANO
Breslau, 1909

[After 12 Q–B3?]

	WHITE	BLACK			
	A. Lasker	E. Lasker			
1	P–K4	P–K4			
2	Kt–KB3	Kt–QB3			
3	B–B4	Kt–B3			
4	P–Q3	B–B4			
5	B–KKt5	P–Q3			
6	P–KR3	B–K3			
7	B–Kt5	P–QR3			
8	B × Kt*ch*	P × B [*a*]	14	Q × R*ch*	K–Q2
9	P–Q4	P × P	15	Q × R	Q–B8*ch* [*e*]
10	Kt × P	B × Kt [*b*]	16	K–K2	Q × P*ch*
11	Q × B	P–B4	17	K–K3	Q × P*ch!* [*f*]
12	Q–B3? [*c*]*	Kt × P*!*	18	K–Q3	P–B5*ch*
13	Q × KtP? [*d*]	Q × B*!!*	19	K × Kt	P–B4 *mate* [*g*]

[*a*] Thus far the course of the game has been quite tranquil; but now it livens up.

[*b*] 10 ... B–Q2 is the move to preserve the two Bishops, but Black apparently does not want to lose time.

[*c*] 12 Q–K3 was safe and sane. The more adventurous text turns out badly.

[*d*] White is under the impression that his opponent has fallen into a trap; actually, we are about to meet our old friend, the two-Rook sacrifice. White's relatively best course was 13 B×Q, Kt×Q; 14 B×P, Kt×Kt; 15 R×Kt, K–Q2; 16 B–R5, B×QRP; 17 R–R1, B–Q4 and Black's material advantage may be nullified by the Bishops of opposite color.

[*e*] Now it's Black's turn!

[*f*] The pretty point of the combination: if 18 K×Kt, B–B4*ch*; 19 K–Q5, Q–Q5 *mate*.

[*g*] Had White played 15 Q×P, the conclusion at move 19 would be: 19 ... P–Q4*ch*; 20 K–K5, Q–K6*ch*; 21 K–B6, Q–B5*ch*; 22 K–Kt7, Q–Kt4*ch* and mate next move.

HEALTHY SKEPTICISM

WORLD CHAMPION EMANUÈL LASKER was primarily an empiricist who preferred to judge every position on its merits. He generally ignored formal opening theory because of his skeptical attitude toward academic analysis. Time and again he proved in his games that a piece of far-reaching analysis could not stand the test of practical application.

When, therefore, Lasker's own analysis was brusquely refuted by Reti in this attractive little game, Lasker must have been pleased, even if the joke was on him!

RUY LOPEZ

Match, 1910

[After 18 R × B]

WHITE	BLACK
R. Reti	K. Sterk

	WHITE	BLACK
1	P–K4	P–K4
2	Kt–KB3	Kt–QB3
3	B–Kt5	Kt–B3
4	O–O	P–Q3 [a]
5	P–Q4	B–Q2
6	Kt–B3	B–K2
7	B–Kt5	P × P
8	Kt × P	O–O
9	B × QKt	P × B [b]
10	Q–Q3	Kt–Kt5 [c]
11	B × B	Q × B
12	P–B4	P–KB4 [d]
13	QR–K1! [e]	P × P [f]
14	Kt × KP	Q–R5
15	P–KR3	Kt–B3 [g]
16	Kt–KKt5!	P–Q4 [h]
17	Kt(5)–K6!	B × Kt [i]
18	R × B*	P–B4 [j]
19	Kt–B5	Q–R4
20	R × Kt!!	Resigns [k]

[*a*] It is curious that although the Steinitz Defense has been condemned for its passive qualities, it has been a prime favorite with three World Champions: Steinitz, Lasker, Capablanca.

[*b*] Hoping for ... Kt × P, which White prevents.

[*c*] As Black's two Bishops are of little value in his congested position, he prefers to part with one of them in the hope of improving his position.

[*d*] Premature, as White is the first to occupy the King file.

[*e*] The capture of the KBP leads to nothing: 13 P × P, Q–K6*ch*; 14 Q × Q, Kt × Q; 15 KR–K1, Kt × KBP (or even 15 ... P–B4*!*); or else 13 Kt × KBP, B × Kt; 14 P × B, Q–K6*ch*; 15 Q × Q, Kt × Q etc.

[*f*] Schlechter–Havasi, Kaschau, 1918, continued: 13 ... Q–B2; 14 P–KR3, P × P; 15 Kt × KP, Kt–B3; 16 Kt–KKt5, Q–Q4; 17 P–B4*!*, Q–R4; 18 R–K7, KR–Q1; 19 Kt × RP*!*, *resigns.*

[*g*] Thus far the game has followed analysis by Lasker, who concluded that the game was even.

[*h*] No matter how Black plays, White occupies K6 with decisive effect.

[*i*] Or 17 ... KR–B1; 18 Kt–KB5 and wins.

[*j*] Black is lost. If 18 ... Kt–K5; 19 R × P, R × P; 20 R × P, R × R*ch*; 21 Q × R (threatening mate in two with 22 Q–B7*ch* etc., with 22 R × P*ch!* as a subsidiary threat), Q–R4 (if 21 ... R–KB1; 22 R × P*ch!*); 22 Kt–K6 and wins.

[*k*] For if 20 ... P × R (if 20 ... R × R; 21 Q × P*ch* etc.); 21 Q–Kt3*ch*, K–B2 (if 21 ... Q–Kt3; 22 Kt–K7*ch*); 22 Q–Kt7*ch*, K–K3; 23 Q–K7*ch*, K × Kt; 24 P–Kt4*ch* winning the Queen.

NOBLESSE OBLIGE

EVERY OPENING HAS ITS INNER LOGIC, and the ensuing middle game must be conducted along the lines called for by the preceding opening moves. If you play a gambit, you must follow it up energetically to maintain the initiative. To discard the offensive in favor of picking up a stray Pawn, as White does in this game, is to court disaster. White's lapse is aggravated by the fact that his Pawn-snatching opens up an attacking line for the enemy. Black's refutation is as incisive as it is elegant.

KING'S GAMBIT

Abbazia, 1912

*[After 16 ... B–Kt4!]

WHITE	BLACK
M. Lowtzky	G. Nyholm
1 P–K4	P–K4
2 P–KB4	P × P
3 Kt–KB3	Kt–KB3
4 Kt–B3	P–Q4
5 P–K5	Kt–R4
6 P–Q4	P–KKt4 [a]
7 B–K2	P–Kt5
8 O–O!	R–Kt1! [b]
9 Kt–K1	B–R3
10 B–Q3	B–K3
11 B × RP? [c]	R–R1 [d]
12 Q–Q3	Kt–QB3
13 P–QR3 [e]	Q–R5 [f]
14 B–B5	O–O–O
15 B × Bch	P × B

16 Kt–R4	B–Kt4! [g]*
17 P–R3 [h]	P × P
18 Q × P	Kt–Kt6
19 R–B2 [i]	Q–Kt5!! [j]
20 R × P	B × R!
Resigns [k]	

[52]

[*a*] Black's defense is a curious blend of modern (... Kt–KB3) and old-fashioned (... P–KKt4) elements.

[*b*] Quite right: after 8 ... P×Kt; 9 KB×P, Kt–Kt2; 10 Kt×P White would have the makings of a savage attack.

[*c*] Up to this point White has played well, but here he goes astray. The right move was 11 Kt–K2! winning the valuable gambit Pawn and remaining with a fine game after the opening of the King's Bishop file.

[*d*] Now Black rejoices in the possession of an open King's Rook file, which, though momentarily blocked, will be put to good use later on. White has repeated Dufresne's mistake (see page 8).

[*e*] Or 13 B–B5, Q–R5; 14 B×B, P×B; 15 Q–Kt6*ch*, K–K2 and Black has all the play.

[*f*] 13 ... Kt×QP was also possible, but Black, unlike his opponent, is interested in attack.

[*g*] Threatening 16 ... Kt–Kt6!

[*h*] Hopeless. But in the event of 17 Kt–B5 Black could even play 17 ... Kt×QP, for if 18 Q×Kt, Q×P*ch!!*; 19 K×Q (if 19 K–B2, B–R5*ch*; 20 K–K2, Kt–Kt6*ch* and 21 K–B2 is impossible because of 21 ... Kt–B4*ch*), Kt–Kt6*ch*; 20 K–Kt1, R–R8*ch*; 21 K–B2, R×R *mate*.

[*i*] If 19 Q×Q, R×Q wins at least a Rook.

[*j*] Black can win as he pleases, and he pleases to win very prettily. Of course, if 20 Q×Q, R–R8 *mate*.

[*k*] If 21 Q×Q, R–R8*ch*; 22 K–B2, R–B8 *mate*.

MULTUM IN PARVO

THIS GAME IS PERHAPS the most complicated contest of its length that has ever been played. Certainly no game produced by the old masters with this opening can vie in tactical intricacy with this thrilling struggle, fought out under the usual modern time limit. We readily forgive the players their miscalculations, and offer them our thanks for producing such a delightful game, which truly contains "much in little."

BISHOP'S GAMBIT
Abbazia, 1912

[After 12 ... Q–Kt4!!]

WHITE	BLACK
A. Flamberg	O. Duras

1 P–K4	P–K4
2 P–KB4	P×P
3 B–B4	Kt–QB3
4 P–Q4	Kt–B3!
5 P–K5	P–Q4!
6 B–K2	Kt–K5
7 B×P	P–B3!
8 Kt–KB3	P×P
9 Kt×P	Kt×Kt
10 B×Kt	B–Kt5ch!
11 P–B3	O–O! [a]
12 B–B3	Q–Kt4!!*
13 Kt–Q2 [b]	R×B!

14 P×R [c]	Q–R5ch		
15 K–K2	Q–B7ch		
16 K–Q3	Kt×Kt? [d]		
17 P×B? [e]	Kt–B5!		
	Resigns [f]		

[a] Beginning a strong attack. If 12 P×B, Kt–B7 etc.

[b] White's best chance was 13 P×B, forcing Black to take
a draw by 13 ... Q–K6*ch*; 14 Q–K2, Q–B8*ch*; 15
Q–Q1, Q–K6*ch* etc. If Black tries to win with 15 ...
Q×P?; 16 Kt–Q2, Kt×Kt (or 16 ... R×B?!;
17 P×R, Kt×Kt; 18 Q×Kt!, Q×R*ch*; 19 K–B2,
Q×R; 20 Q–Kt5, P–KKt3; 21 Q–K7 wins); 17
Q×Kt!, Q×R*ch*; 18 K–K2, Q×R; 19 Q–Kt5,
P–KKt3 (if 19 ... R–B2; 20 Q–Q8*ch*, R–B1; 21
B×P*ch*, B–K3; 22 B×B*ch*, K–R1; 23 B×P*ch!*
etc.); 20 Q–K7 wins.
13 B×Kt is not good, for example 13 ... P×B;
14 Q–Kt3*ch* (if 14 Q–Q2, P–K6!; or 14 Q–K2,
B–Kt5!; 15 Q–B4*ch*, K–R1 etc.; or 14 P–KKt3,
B–Kt5; 15 B–B4, R×B!!; 16 Q–Q2, P–K6!; 17
Q×P, R–K5!; 18 Q×R, Q–B8*ch* with a mating
attack; or 14 R–B1, Q–K6*ch*; 15 Q–K2, Q–B8*ch*
and wins), K–R1; 15 P×B (15 Q×B?? allows mate in
two!), Q×P; 16 B×P*ch*, K×B; 17 Q–Kt3*ch*,
Q×Q*ch* with a winning endgame.

[c] Or 14 Kt×R, Q×P; 15 R–KB1, Kt×P; 16 Q–Q3,
B–KB4; 17 Q–K3, Kt–Q8*ch*; 18 K×Kt, Q–B7 *mate.*

[d] 16 ... Kt–B4*ch!!* wins: 17 P×Kt forced, B–B4*ch*;
18 Kt–K4, P×Kt*ch*; 19 P×P, R–Q1*ch*; 20 B–Q4,
B×P(B4)!; 21 Q–Kt3*ch*, K–R1; 22 P×B, B×B;
23 K–B4, B–Kt3! etc.

[e] Of course not 17 Q×Kt??, B–B4 *mate!* But 17 Q–K2!!
wins: 17 ... Kt–K5!; 18 QR–KB1! (not 18 P×Kt??,
P×P*ch*; 19 Q×P, B–KB4 nor 19 K–Q2, P–K6*ch*;
20 K–Q1, B–Kt5! Or 18 P×B?, B–B4! regaining the
exchange), Q×Q*ch*; 19 K×Q, Kt×P*ch*; 20 P×Kt,
B×P; 21 KR–Kt1!, P–KKt3; 22 R–B1 etc.

[f] Mate or ruinous loss of material is unavoidable.

"THE UNQUIET GAME"

FOR ALL OUR RESPECTFUL FAMILIARITY with Nimzovich's remarkable tactical dexterity, this game strikes us as an exceptional performance. The number and intensity of sharp complications which this game conjures up in only 17 moves are truly astonishing.

Even more surprising, perhaps, is the fact that all this happens after what is proverbially a tranquil and sometimes lifeless opening. In the hands of a genius like Nimzovich, the Giuoco Piano ("the quiet game") becomes "the unquiet game." Mediocrity (see Fleissig–Schlechter, page 26) restlessly seeks the exotic; genius unearths the exotic even in the familiar and well-worn patterns.

GIUOCO PIANO
Correspondence, 1913

*[After 14 ... KP × P]

WHITE	BLACK		
A. Nimzovich	Dr. G. Fluess		
1 P–K4	P–K4		
2 Kt–KB3	Kt–QB3		
3 Kt–B3	Kt–B3		
4 B–B4	B–B4		
5 P–Q3	P–Q3		
6 B–KKt5	P–KR3		
7 B–R4	P–KKt4!?		
8 B–KKt3	B–KKt5		
9 P–KR4	Kt–KR4 [a]		
10 P × P?	Kt–Q5? [b]	14 P–B4!	KP × P [f]*
11 B × P! [c]	B × Kt [d]	15 Q–Kt4!!	Kt × Pch
12 P × B	P × B	16 K–Q2	Kt × R [g]
13 R × Kt	KR–Kt1 [e]	17 B × Pch!	Resigns [h]

[56]

[*a*] Black has driven off the annoying Bishop, but at the cost of weakening his position. Nimzovich recommends 10 Kt–Q5, Kt–Q5; 11 P–B3 as White's proper procedure.

[*b*] Correct, says Nimzovich, was 10 ... Kt×B*!*; 11 P×Kt, Kt–Q5 so that if 12 Kt–Q5, B×Kt; 13 P×B, Q×P*!*; 14 P–KKt4 (if 14 Kt×P*ch*, K–Q2; 15 Kt×R, Q–K6*ch* and wins), P–QB3*!*; 15 R–R5, P×Kt*!*; 16 R×Q, P×R and wins!

[*c*] Having been spared, the Bishop becomes obnoxious!

[*d*] If 11 ... P×B; 12 B×P*ch!* etc.

[*e*] White is in trouble, for if 14 R×P, Q×P; 15 R–R1 Q–Kt7. But Nimzovich has a way out!

[*f*] If 14 ... Q–Q2 (to prevent White's next move); 15 Kt–Q5*!* is very strong.

[*g*] With a Rook down, Nimzovich has another sacrifice!

[*h*] For if 17 ... K×B (or 17 ... K–B1; 18 B×R, K×B; 19 P×P*ch* and wins); 18 Q–B5*ch*, K–K1 (if 18 ... K–K2; 19 Kt–Q5*ch* or 18 ... K–Kt2; 19 R×P and wins); 19 Q–K6*ch*, Q–Q2 (if 19 ... K–B1; 20 P–Kt6 wins); 20 Q×R*ch*, Q–B1; 21 Q–R7, Q–K2; 22 P–Kt6, Q×Q (if 22 ... B–Q5; 23 Kt–Kt5*!*, Q–Kt5*ch*; 24 K–Q1 etc.); 23 P×Q, B–Q5; 24 Kt–Kt5*!* and wins! A fascinating game.

GREEN WHISKERS

THERE IS DOUBTFUL WISDOM and little practical value in the platitude that a bad plan is better than no plan at all. This is effectively illustrated here by the drastic sequel to Black's adoption of a bad plan.

A comical note is introduced by the wanderings of Hrdina's Knight, whose futility reminds us of his colleague in *Through the Looking Glass:*

> "But I was thinking of a plan
> To dye one's whiskers green,
> And always use so large a fan
> That they could not be seen."

FOUR KNIGHTS'
GAME

Prague, 1913

*[After 14 P–B5!!]

WHITE	BLACK
K. Opocensky	J. Hrdina
1 P–K4	P–K4
2 Kt–KB3	Kt–QB3
3 Kt–B3	Kt–B3
4 B–Kt5	B–Kt5
5 O–O	O–O
6 P–Q3	P–Q3
7 B–Kt5	Kt–K2 [a]
8 Kt–KR4	P–B3
9 B–QB4	Kt–Kt3
10 Kt×Kt	P×Kt
11 P–B4 [b]	Q–Kt3ch?
12 K–RI	Kt–Kt5
13 Q–KI	Kt–K6 [c]

14 P–B5!! [d]*	Kt×B [e]
15 P–B6!! [f]	B–Kt5 [g]
16 Q–R4	B–KR4
17 P–Kt4	Kt–K6 [h]
18 P×B	Kt×R [i]
19 P–R6!!	Resigns [j]

[58]

[a] 7 ... B×Kt is more customary, but, as will be seen, Black can put the Bishop to good use.

[b] The logical move: he wants to open the Bishop file to put more pressure on Black's Knight. However, Black can extricate himself with 11 ... B–B4*ch!* (see the previous note); 12 K–R1, B–K6*!*; 13 Q–B3, B×P; 14 B×B, P×B; 15 Q×P, Q–K2 with a fairly level game.

[c] The move that Black relied on: the double attack on Bishop and Rook will ensure the removal of the KB.

[d] Opocensky sees further into the position. His concentration of force against the King-side enables him to ignore the superficial, not to say frivolous, Knight moves.

[e] Necessary, for if 14 ... Kt×R; 15 P×P (threatening to win outright with 16 Q–R4), P–Q4; 16 Q–R4, P×KtP; 17 P×P, P×P (or 17 ... Kt–K6; 18 B×Kt, Q×B; 19 P–Q6*ch*, R–B2; 20 Q–Q8*ch* etc.); 18 Kt×P and wins!

[f] White is weaving a mating net; he disdains to pick up the errant Knight.

[g] If 15 ... P×P; 16 B×P followed by Q–R4–8 *mate*. Amusing is 15 ... B×Kt; 16 Q–R4, B–Q7; 17 P×P*!*, K×P; 18 B–B6*ch* and mate next move.

[h] The Knight huffs and puffs in his fidgety efforts to play an important role.

[i] "*Now* will you look at me?!" But White goes brusquely for the mate.

[j] The threat is 20 RP×P and 21 Q–R8 *mate*. Either 19 ... P×BP or P×RP allows a quick mate.

[59]

GENERAL PRINCIPLES

IT WOULD BE TOO MUCH to ask of the reader that he be able to foresee the consequences of White's sacrifice of two Rooks and a Knight. That is where general principles prove their utility. They tell us that with Black's Queen completely out of play and his forces undeveloped, his lone King has little chance of survival.

And so it turns out. But this game is not a dry demonstration of an abstract proposition. It is played with that combination of elegance and precision which makes Morphy's games so rewarding to study.

DUTCH DEFENSE

Correspondence, 1915

WHITE	BLACK
R. Edgar	T. Lott

[After 8 Q–R5ch!]

	WHITE	BLACK
1	P–Q4	P–KB4
2	P–K4	P×P
3	Kt–QB3	Kt–KB3
4	B–KKt5	P–K3
5	B×Kt	Q×B
6	Kt×P	Q–Kt3?
7	B–Q3!	Q×P?
8	Q–R5ch! [a]*	P–Kt3
9	Q–K5!	Q×R
10	Q×R	Q×Ktch
11	K–Q2	Q×R
12	Kt–B6ch [b]	K–K2 [c]
13	Kt–Q5ch!!	P×Kt [d]
14	Q×Pch	K–Q3
15	Q×KtPch	K–K2
16	Q–Kt5ch	K–B2 [e]
17	B–Kt6ch	K–Kt1 [f]
18	Q–B6!!	B–Kt5ch
19	P–B3!!	Resigns [g]

[a] Black is lost! Thus if 8 ... K–Q1; 9 Kt–Kt5, Q×R (if 9 ... P–Kt 3; 10 B×P, P×B; 11 Q×R, K–K2; 12 Q–R7ch, K–B3; 13 Kt[1]–B3!, Q×Rch; 14 K–K2, Q×R; 15 Q–B7 mate); 10 Kt–B7ch, K–K2; 11 Kt×R, Q×Ktch; 12 K–K2, Q×R; 13 Q–B7ch, K–Q3; 14 Q×Bch and 15 Q–B5 mate!
Or 8 ... K–K2; 9 Q–R4ch, K–K1 (9 ... P–Kt4; 10 Kt×P, Q×R; 11 Kt×RPch, K–Q3; 12 Q–B4ch is disastrous for Black); 10 Kt–Kt3, Q–B3 (else 11 B–K4); 11 B×P, R×B; 12 Q×R and White wins without much trouble.

[b] Now it's White's turn!

[c] Or 12 ... K–B2; 13 Q×Pch, K×Kt; 14 Q×Pch, K–K2; 15 Q–Kt5ch, K–B2 (if 15 ... K–Q3; 16 Q–B5 mate); 16 B–Kt6ch and wins (see note [f]).

[d] If 13 ... K–K1; 14 Q×P, P×Kt; 15 B×Pch, K–Q1; 16 Q–R4ch and mate in two more moves.

[e] If 16 ... K–Q3; 17 Q–B6 mate!—and if 16 ... K–K3; 17 B–B5ch forces the text position.

[f] If 17 ... K–K3; 18 Q–K5 mate; if 17 ... K–Kt2; 18 B–K8ch, K–R1; 19 Q–R5ch, K–Kt2; 20 Q–B7ch followed by a quick mate.

[g] For after 19 ... Q×Pch; 20 K–Q1!, Q–R8ch; 21 K–K2!, Q–Kt7ch; 22 K–B3!, Q×QBPch; 23 K–Kt2! the checks are over. A great game!

THE LESSON OF THE MASTER

EVERY MODERN PLAYER of note has learned much, directly or indirectly, from the works of Siegbert Tarrasch. The most important lesson offered by Tarrasch was his impressive demonstration of how to utilize superior mobility. "Congested positions," runs his most famous maxim, "have the germ of defeat in them." Tarrasch turned this type of position play into a standardized process that could be applied over and over again, taught to and learned by thousands of players. Tarrasch put chess theory on the conveyor belt.

FRENCH DEFENSE

Match, 1916

[After 16 Q–R3!]

WHITE	BLACK
Dr. S.	*J.*
Tarrasch	*Mieses*

1	P–K4	P–K3	
2	P–Q4	P–Q4	
3	Kt–QB3	P×P [a]	
4	Kt×P	Kt–Q2	
5	Kt–KB3	KKt–B3	
6	B–Q3	B–K2	
7	O–O	Kt×Kt	
8	B×Kt	Kt–B3	
9	B–Q3	P–QKt3? [b]	15 KR–K1	KR–K1 [h]
10	Kt–K5!	O–O [c]	16 Q–R3!*	Q–Q3 [i]
11	Kt–B6	Q–Q3	17 B×Kt	P×B
12	Q–B3! [d]	B–Q2 [e]	18 Q–R6! [j]	P–KB4
13	Kt×Bch	Q×Kt	19 R–K3	Q×P [k]
14	B–KKt5 [f]	QR–B1 [g]	20 P–QB3!	Resigns [l]

[*a*] Deliberate provocation! This defense gives White a much freer game: why play it against the virtuoso of such positions? (See also Strautmanis–Hasenfuss, page 110.)

[*b*] A trouble-maker. 9 ... P–B4 is the best bid for freedom.

[*c*] Allowing a powerful invasion by White's advanced Knight. But 10 ... B–Kt2; 11 B–Kt5*ch*, K–B1; 12 B–B6 is even drearier for Black.

[*d*] The more obvious 12 Kt×B*ch*, Q×Kt; 13 Q–B3, R–Kt1 followed by ... B–Kt2 gives Black a fair game.

[*e*] 12 ... B–Kt2? loses a piece by 13 Kt×B*ch* etc. If 12 ... Kt–Q4?; 13 Kt×B*ch*, Q×Kt; 14 P–B4 wins material.

[*f*] Tarrasch holds all the positional trumps and has good attacking chances. He threatens 15 Q–K4! forcing a serious weakness (15 ... P–Kt3), for if 15 ... Kt×Q?; 16 B×Q winning at least the exchange (15 ... KR–K1??; 16 B×Kt etc.).

[*g*] *Now* he can answer 15 Q–K4 with 15 ... Kt×Q (why?!).

[*h*] 15 ... P–KR3 should have been tried, although Black would have been very uncomfortable after 16 B–R4.

[*i*] He had no good reply to the threatened 17 B×Kt and 18 Q×P*ch*. Thus if 16 ... P–K4?; 17 B×Kt! wins a piece! Or 16 ... P–Kt3; 17 Q–R4, K–Kt2; 18 R–K4 and 19 R–B4 winning. If 16 ... P–KR3; 17 B×P, P×B; 18 Q×RP followed by 19 R–K5 or 19 R–K3 etc.

[*j*] Threatening 19 B×P*ch* followed by mate in three.

[*k*] Hoping for 20 R–Kt3*ch*, K–R1; 21 P–B3, Q–K4; but even then 22 P–KB4, Q–B4*ch*; 23 K–R1, Q–B1; 24 Q–B6*ch* leads to mate.

[*l*] He can stop mate only by giving up the Queen.

THE STILETTO

I N MODERN MASTER GAMES the fianchetto has come to play an all-important role. The King fianchetto (at KKt2) is directed against the center and the hostile Queen-side, and has, therefore, a predominantly strategic significance. The Queen fianchetto (at QKt2) aims, however, at the center and *at the King-side as well*. In the hands of a skilful attacking player, the Queen fianchetto has all the menace of a stiletto poised against the very heart of the enemy's position.

Many years ago, Rubinstein played an immortal game against Rotlevi, the basic motif being the power of his Queen's Bishop on the long diagonal. In the following game, played about ten years later, Rubinstein echoed this theme.

FOUR KNIGHTS' GAME

Warsaw, 1917

*[After 14 ... P–KR4!]

WHITE	BLACK
J.	*A.*
Belsitzmann	*Rubinstein*

	WHITE	BLACK		WHITE	BLACK
1	P–K4	P–K4			
2	Kt–KB3	Kt–QB3			
3	Kt–B3	Kt–B3			
4	B–Kt5	Kt–Q5! [*a*]			
5	B–B4	B–B4			
6	Kt×P	Q–K2! [*b*]	12	Kt–K1	Q–R5! [*e*]
7	Kt–Q3? [*c*]	P–Q4!	13	P–Kt3	Q–R6
8	Kt×P	Q×P*ch*	14	P–QB3	P–KR4! [*f*]*
9	Kt–K3	B–Q3	15	P×Kt	P–R5! [*g*]
10	O–O	P–QKt4! [*d*]	16	Q–K2	Q×RP*ch!!*
11	B–Kt3	B–Kt2		Resigns [*h*]	

[64]

[*a*] Rubinstein's favorite means of taking the sting out of this opening. If now 5 Kt×P, Q–K2; 6 P–B4, Kt×B; 7 Kt×Kt, P–Q3 and Black stands well.

[*b*] Black has sacrificed a Pawn to get a big lead in development. He does not fear 7 Kt×BP because of 7 ... P–Q4*!*; 8 Kt×R, P×B etc.

[*c*] Leads to intolerable congestion. The normal-looking 7 Kt–B3 was better.

[*d*] Masterly play: without loss of time he posts his Queen's Bishop on the long diagonal.

[*e*] Forcing the advance of White's KKtP (if 13 P–KR3, Q–B5 and 14 P–KKt3 must be played), after which the power of Black's fianchettoed Bishop is greatly enhanced.

[*f*] Rubinstein does not bother to retreat the Knight, as he is planning a magnificently timed finish.

[*g*] White has no defense against the coming sacrifice. Thus if 16 P–B3, P×P; 17 Q–K2, P×P*ch*; 18 K–R1, Kt–R4*!*; 19 Kt–B5*ch*, K–B1; 20 R–B2, R–K1; 21 Q–B1, R×Kt*!*; 22 Q×R, Q×P*ch!*; 23 R×Q, B×R *mate!*

[*h*] If 17 K×Q, P×P*ch*; 18 K–Kt1, R–R8 *mate!* Triumph of the long diagonal.

WHAT'S IN A NAME?

THERE ARE SOME OPENINGS whose very name conjure up a vision of slashing attacks, brilliant sacrifices, surprises at every turn. The Max Lange Attack is such an opening, and the following game is the *beau ideal* of the Max Lange.

Admirers of elegant combination play will be pleased with the triple illustration of the same beautiful Queen sacrifice.

MAX LANGE
ATTACK

London, 1918

WHITE	BLACK
C. W. Brown	*F. Gibbs*
1 P–K4	P–K4
2 Kt–KB3	Kt–QB3
3 B–B4	B–B4
4 O–O	Kt–B3
5 P–Q4	P × P
6 P–K5	P–Q4
7 P × Kt	P × B
8 R–K1 *ch*	K–B1 [*a*]
9 B–Kt5!	P × P [*b*]
10 B–R6 *ch*	K–Kt1
11 Kt–B3! [*c*]	B–KKt5 [*d*]

[After 13 Q–K2!]

12 Kt–K4	B–Kt3? [*e*]
13 Q–K2! [*f*]*	Kt–K4 [*g*]
14 Kt × Kt!!!	B × Q
15 Kt–Q7!!!	Resigns [*h*]

[*a*] The usual continuation is 8 ... B–K3; 9 Kt–Kt5, Q–Q4; 10 Kt–QB3, Q–B4; 11 QKt–K4 with a complicated middle game which will tax the ingenuity of both players. Black therefore tries something "simpler"; but, as is customary when castling has been forfeited, Black's King will have to accustom himself to a certain amount of persecution.

[*b*] White was threatening to win the Queen with 10 P × P*ch*. 9 ... P–KKt3? loses the exchange (10 B–R6*ch*, K–Kt1; 11 B–Kt7).

[*c*] A game Teichmann–Wolf (played where?, when?) continued 11 Kt × P!, B × Kt (if 11 ... Kt × Kt; 12 P–QB3. If 11 ... Q × Kt??; 12 R–K8*ch* leads to mate); 12 P–B3, B–K3; 13 P × B, Q × P; 14 Q–R5, Kt–K4; 15 Kt–B3, Q–Kt5; 16 R × Kt!, P × R; 17 Kt–Q5!, *resigns*!

[*d*] 11 ... P × Kt?? is refuted by 12 Q × Q*ch*, Kt × Q; 13 R–K8*ch* and mate next move. *Practical Chess Openings* recommends 11 ... B–B1, giving the pedestrian 12 B × B in reply. However, a game Mueller–Bauer, 1907, went 11 ... B–B1; 12 Kt × P!, Kt × Kt? (if 12 ... Q × Kt?; 13 R–K8, Q–B4; 14 Kt–K4 wins. On 12 ... B × B; 13 Kt × Kt, Q × Q; 14 Kt–K7*ch* yields White a favorable ending); 13 Q × Kt!, B–KB4; 14 Q–KB4, B × P (apparently to stop 15 QR–Q1); 15 QR–Q1!, B–Q3 (if 15 ... B × R; 16 Q–Kt3*ch* forces mate); 16 Kt–Q5!!, B × R; 17 R–K8*ch*, Q × R; 18 Kt × P *mate*!

[*e*] But here the only chance was 12 ... B–KB1.

[*f*] Threatening mate in three with 14 Kt × P*ch*!, Q × Kt; 15 Q–K8*ch*! etc.

[*g*] Allows a startling reply.

[*h*] He cannot stop mate by 16 Kt × P*ch* etc.

CHESS BY MAIL

IN RECENT YEARS, correspondence chess has gained a great many new devotees. Thousands of players find it their only means of active participation in chess. All the venerable prejudices against correspondence play have died out: it is recognized as a splendid means of schooling oneself in the fine points of opening, middle game and end game. Many are the delightful brilliancies which this supposedly sedate form of chess has given us. Here is one example which surely deserves the adjective "unforgettable":

SICILIAN DEFENSE   *[After 13 ... P–Q3]*

Correspondence, 1920

WHITE	BLACK
J. Brunnemer	*Failing*
1 P–K4	P–QB4
2 Kt–KB3	Kt–QB3
3 P–Q4	P × P
4 Kt × P	Kt–B3
5 Kt–QB3	P–K3
6 B–K2	B–Kt5
7 O–O*!?*	B × Kt
8 P × B	Kt × P
9 B–B3 [*a*]	Kt × QBP*?*
10 Q–Q3	Kt–Q4 [*b*]
11 B × Kt	P × B
12 R–K1*ch*	K–B1
13 Kt–B5	P–Q3*

14 Kt × KtP*!*	Kt–K4 [*c*]
15 Kt–R5*!!*	B–K3 [*d*]
16 R × Kt*!*	P × R
17 B–R3*ch*	K–K1
18 Q–Kt5*ch*	Resigns [*e*]

[*a*] Black should now play 9 ... P–Q4, instead of greedily snapping at another Pawn.

[*b*] The position offers many possibilities for pretty play, for example: 10 ... Kt–R5; 11 B–R3, P–QR3; 12 Kt–B5!, Q–B3; 13 B×Kt, KtP×B; 14 Kt–Q6*ch*, K–Q1; 15 Q–QKt3!, *resigns* (Tenner–Richter, 1911). Another instance: 10 ... Kt×Kt; 11 Q×Kt(4), Q–B3; 12 Q–QKt4, Kt–Q4; 13 B×Kt, Q×R; 14 B–Kt2, Q×R*ch*; 15 K×Q, P–QR4; 16 Q–Q6!, P×B; 17 B–R3, K–Q1; 18 Q–Kt6*ch*, K–K1; 19 Q–K3*ch*, K–Q1; 20 B–K7*ch*, K–B2; 21 Q–B5*ch*, *resigns* (Alexander–Sergeant, London, 1939).

[*c*] White has begun a magnificent sacrificial sequence. If 14 ... K×Kt; 15 Q–Kt3*ch*, K–B1; 16 B–R6 *mate!*

[*d*] If 15 ... Kt×Q; 16 B–R6*ch*, K–Kt1; 17 R–K8*ch!*, Q×R; 18 Kt–B6 *mate*. Or 15 ... P–KR3; 16 R×Kt!, P×R; 17 Q–KKt3, R–R2; 18 B–R3*ch* and wins.

[*e*] The decision has come from the other wing! If 18 ... B–Q2 (18 ... Q–Q2; 19 Kt–B6*ch*); 19 Kt–Kt7 *mate*.

THE POWER OF THE PIN

HE PIN IS PERHAPS THE STRONGEST and most common of all tactical motifs. It is, fortunately, also one of the easiest to understand and apply. Its undoubted power over the enemy's pieces results in a psychological advantage as well: nothing is so depressing as being subjected to an irritating pin which gives every indication of being permanent. It is a death sentence for one's pieces.

As far as the aggressor is concerned, the pin has a psychological effect of a different kind. Being a valuable asset, the pin gives him a feeling of confidence in his game and often forms the basis of a winning plan.

QUEEN'S INDIAN DEFENSE

Budapest, 1921

*[After 12 B–Kt5!]

	WHITE	BLACK
	B. Kostich	A. Steiner
1	P–Q4	Kt–KB3
2	Kt–KB3	P–QKt3
3	P–KKt3	B–Kt2
4	B–Kt2	P–Kt3? [a]
5	O–O? [b]	B–Kt2?
6	P–B4	O–O [c]
7	Kt–B3	P–Q3? [d]
8	Q–B2	QKt–Q2
9	R–Q1! [e]	R–K1
10	P–K4	P–K4?
11	P×P	P×P [f]
12	B–Kt5!*	P–B3 [g]
13	B×Kt! [h]	B×B
14	B–R3!	R–K2 [i]
15	R–Q6	Q–B2 [j]
16	QR–Q1	R–Q1 [k]
17	Q–Q2!	B–B1 [l]
18	R×B!	Resigns

[*a*] 4 ... P–B4*!* gives Black an easy game, 5 P–Q5 being impossible.

[*b*] More exact 5 P–B4*!*, so that if 5 ... P–B4; 6 P–Q5 and Black's position is very cramped.

[*c*] Now it is too late for ... P–B4 (7 P–Q5*!*).

[*d*] It is clear that Black's position will be constricted. He should therefore try to free himself somewhat with 7 ... Kt–K5. See White's next move!

[*e*] Preventing the intended 9 ... P–K4 (why?).

[*f*] Running into a disastrous pin; but if 11 ... QKt×P*?*; 12 Kt×Kt, R×Kt; 13 B–B4, R–K1; 14 P–K5*!* winning a piece!

[*g*] To stop Kt–Q5; but meanwhile he creates a point of invasion for White at Q6. 12 ... P–KR3 is no help, for after 13 B×Kt, B×B; 14 B–R3 Black has the same kind of troubles as after the text.

[*h*] Strengthens the pin on the remaining Knight.

[*i*] After 14 ... B–B1; 15 R–Q6, B–K2 White can win a Pawn with 16 B×Kt*!*, B×R (or 16 ... B×B; 17 R–Q2, Q–B2; 18 Kt×P*!*); 17 B×P*!* etc.

[*j*] If 15 ... B–Kt2; 16 QR–Q1, B–QB1; 17 Q–Q2 winning a piece!

[*k*] A trap: if 17 B×Kt, R(2)×B; 18 R×B*?*, R×R*ch*; 19 Kt×R, K–Kt2 and the Rook has no escape!

[*l*] The loss of a piece was unavoidable.

ROLLING STONE

HERE THE BLACK KING imitates the antics of his White colleague in the earlier game between Hamppe and Meitner. There the King walked on eggs, slipped through the hostile lines to QB6, and forced his opponent to content himself with a perpetual check! But here the King's forced march is really sinister: he is driven into a mating net.

The utter uselessness of Black's Queen ahead gives the game a rollicking character.

CENTER COUNTER GAME

Correspondence, 1922

WHITE	BLACK
Dr. Imbaud	*Strumilo*

[After 9 Kt × P!!]

	WHITE	BLACK			
1	P–K4	P–Q4			
2	P × P	Kt–KB3			
3	Kt–QB3	Kt × P			
4	B–B4	Kt–Kt3			
5	B–Kt3	Kt–B3 [*a*]			
6	Kt–B3	P–K4			
7	P–Q3	B–KKt5 [*b*]	14	R × B [*g*]	K–K6 [*h*]
8	P–KR3 [*c*]	B–R4??	15	O–O!!	Kt–Q5
9	Kt × P!!*	B × Q [*d*]	16	QR–K1*ch*	Kt–K7*ch*
10	B × P*ch*	K–K2	17	R × Kt*ch!* [*i*]	K × R
11	B–Kt5*ch*	K–Q3 [*e*]	18	B–R5*ch*	K–K6
12	Kt–K4*ch!!*	K × Kt	19	R–B3*ch* [*j*]	K–Q5 [*k*]
13	P–B4 *ch*	K–Q5 [*f*]	20	B–B7!!	Resigns [*l*]

[*a*] Transposing into the Alekhine Defense with 5 ...
P–QB4; 6 P–Q3, P–K3 is a safer course.

[*b*] He should play safe with 7 ... B–K2 and 8 ... O–O.

[*c*] Relatively best is now 8 ... B×Kt; 9 Q×B, Q–Q2
although it leaves White with a very promising game.

[*d*] Black bites; he does not see the combination to its end:
and in any event, 9 ... Kt×Kt leaves him a Pawn
down with no prospects.

[*e*] Now White seems to be at a loss, with the advanced Knight
en prise; but the Queen sacrifice has an astonishing
sequel.

[*f*] If 13 ... K–B4; 14 Kt–Kt3 *mate*.

[*g*] Now the threat is 15 K–K2 and 16 P–B3 *mate*.

[*h*] If 14 ... Q×B; 15 P–B3*ch!*, K–K6; 16 O–O! and
Black's King cannot avoid his fate (chief threat: 17
R–B3*ch*, K–K7; 18 R–Q2*ch*, K–K8; 19 R–B1 *mate!*).

[*i*] Naturally.

[*j*] If now 19 ... K–K7; 20 R–Kt3*ch!*, K–K8; 21 R–K3
mate!

[*k*] Is Black escaping?

[*l*] For if 20 ... B–Kt5; 21 P–B3*ch*, B×P; 22 P×B
mate.

BEAUTY AND THE BEAST

I**T IS HELD IN SOME QUARTERS** that the adoption of such defenses as the French is a cowardly evasion of the problems which arise in the open game. The "soft impeachment" goes on to claim that the open games (such as the Danish, Vienna etc.) are more likely to produce combinations.

The answer, based on a study of master play, is simple: you can avoid some problems, but not all problems. You evade the problems of the Ruy Lopez, for example, in order to cope with the problems of the French Defense. As for beautiful chess, it is even more likely to arise in close games, because exchanges are less frequent in close openings. Maroczy provides a stunning instance.

FRENCH DEFENSE

London, 1923

WHITE	BLACK
Whitehead	*G. Maroczy*
1 P–K4	P–K3
2 P–Q4	P–Q4
3 Kt–QB3	Kt–KB3
4 P–K5	KKt–Q2
5 QKt–K2 [a]	P–QB4 [b]
6 P–QB3	Kt–QB3
7 P–KB4	Q–Kt3
8 Kt–B3	P–B3! [c]
9 P–KKt3	P×QP
10 P×QP	P×P
11 BP×P	B–Kt5ch
12 K–B2? [d]	O–O [e]
13 B–K3 [f]*	Kt(2)×P!!

[After 13 B–K3]

14 P×Kt	R×Ktch!!
15 K×R	Kt×Pch
16 K–B4 [g]	Q–Q3! [h]
17 B–R3 [i]	B–Q2 [j]
18 B–Q4	R–B1ch
Resigns [k]	

[74]

[*a*] White intends to set up a solid center support with P–QB3 and P–KB4. The plan is, however, time-consuming; worse yet, his pieces get in each other's way.

[*b*] The key-move of almost every variation in this defense.

[*c*] White supports his Pawn center, Black harries it.

[*d*] Very dangerous, especially against the wily maestro. 12 Kt–B3 was relatively better, although White's life would be made miserable by the task of guarding the center Pawns.

[*e*] Threatening to capture the KP. Black has a tremendous lead in development, his forces are poised for action.

[*f*] Parries the threat—so he thinks.

[*g*] Black has spent a Rook to demolish the hostile center— and cheap at the price. If White tries 16 K–B2, Kt–Kt5*ch* is deadly: 17 K–Kt1 (17 K–Kt2, Kt×B*ch* or 17 K–B3, Q×B*ch*; 18 K×Kt, P–K4*ch* and mate follows), Q×B*ch*; 18 K–Kt2, Q–K5*ch*; 19 K–Kt1 (or 19 K–R3, Kt–B7 *mate!*), B–B4*ch* etc.

[*h*] White has no defense against 17 ... Q–B1*ch!*; 18 K×Kt (18 K–Kt5 also allows a quick mate), Q–B3 *mate!* Chernev also points out a quick forced mate beginning with 16 ... P–Kt4*ch!*

[*i*] Or 17 B–Q4, Q–B1*ch!*; 18 K–K3, Q–B6 *mate!*

[*j*] Good enough, although 17 ... Q–B1*ch!* is more artistic.

[*k*] For if 19 K–K3, R–B6 *mate.*

[75]

LIGHTNING CHESS

R APID-TRANSIT" OR "BLITZ" CHESS is the modern equivalent of the old-fashioned skittles games. But the modern version has an important advantage over its predecessor: there is a ten-second-per-move time limit. This important provision rules out dawdling on the part of one's opponent.

It is a pity that so few of these quick games have been recorded. They display the modern master's gifts of imagination and improvisation in a really striking manner. The following game, which lasted all of six minutes, is a fair sample.

TWO KNIGHTS'   *[After 13 ... B–B6!]*
DEFENSE

New York, 1923

WHITE	BLACK
O. Field	O. Tenner
1 P–K4	P–K4
2 Kt–KB3	Kt–QB3
3 B–B4	Kt–B3
4 Kt–Kt5	P–Q4
5 P×P	Kt–QR4 [a]
6 P–Q3	P–KR3
7 Kt–KB3	P–K5
8 Q–K2	Kt×B
9 P×Kt	B–QB4
10 KKt–Q2	O–O [b]
11 O–O? [c]	B–KKt5
12 Q–K1	Q–Q2
13 Kt–Kt3	B–B6! [d]*

14 B–B4 [e]	Q–Kt5
15 B–Kt3 [f]	Kt–R4!!
16 Kt×B [g]	Kt–B5!!
17 Kt×KP [h]	Q–R6!! [i]
18 P×Q	Kt×P *mate* [j]

[*a*] 5 ... Kt×P would invite the *Fegatello* ("Fried Liver") Attack (6 Kt×BP*?!*). This line of play is considered inadequate for White, but few players care to submit to its labyrinthine complications.

[*b*] Black's course is clearly indicated: rapid development to compensate for the sacrificed Pawn.

[*c*] This seems natural enough, especially when one studies the "book" variation: 11 Kt–Kt3, B–Kt5; 12 Q–B1, B–Kt5*ch* with a very awkward position for White.

[*d*] White seemed to be on the point of beginning to disentangle himself; but we can see that he suffers from a classic case of "castling into it."

[*e*] He reinforces the King-side after regretfully concluding that he must decline both Bishops. Thus if 14 Kt×B, Q–Kt5 and mate cannot be stopped. Equally painful is 14 P×B, P×P; 15 K–R1 (mate was threatened), Q–R6; 16 R–Kt1, B–Q3; 17 R–Kt3, B×R; 18 Q–Kt1, Kt–Kt5*!*

[*f*] So far, so good. But the attack is still gathering momentum.

[*g*] He can resist everything but temptation—not that he has much choice, as Black was threatening 16 ... Kt×B; 17 P×Kt, Q×P forcing mate! If instead 16 P×B, P×P; 17 K–R1, QR–K1; 18 Q–Q1, Kt×B*ch*; 19 BP×B, R–K7 and there is nothing to be done about ... Q–R6.

[*h*] An exquisite possibility was 17 P×B, Q–R6*!*; 18 B×Kt, P×P and mate follows.

[*i*] At last! Black has been waiting ever since his thirteenth move (a minute and a half ago!) to make this move!

[*j*] Another "Immortal Game."

OPEN AND SHUT

WE GENERALLY THINK of the "open" games (King's Gambit, Evans Gambit etc.) as leading quickly to tactical play, with the "close" games (Queen's Gambit Declined, Dutch Defense etc.) as deferring tactical play for a long time. An examination of actually contested games must, however, modify these assumptions.

Often we find that in the "open" games the quick contact between hostile pieces leads to rapid over-simplification. In the "close" games, such premature contact is postponed, heightening the likelihood of tactical complications. Another characteristic of some "close" games is that they occasionally open up with dizzying speed.

DUTCH DEFENSE

Warsaw, 1924

WHITE	BLACK
D.	J.
Przepiorka	Gottesdiener

*[After 15 ... P × P]

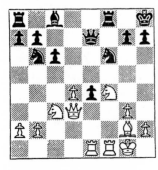

	WHITE	BLACK
1	P–Q4	P–KB4
2	P–KKt3	P–K3
3	B–Kt2	Kt–KB3
4	Kt–KR3! [a]	P–Q4
5	O–O	B–Q3
6	P–QB4	P–B3 [b]
7	Q–Q3	O–O
8	Kt–B3	K–R1
9	B–B4!	B × B
10	Kt × B [c]	Q–K2
11	P–B3	QKt–Q2
12	P × P	KP × P [d]
13	P–K4!	BP × P
14	P × P	Kt–Kt3
15	QR–K1! [e]	P × P*
16	B × P! [f]	Kt × B
17	R × Kt	Q–Q3 [g]
18	R–K5! [h]	Kt–Q2
19	R–KR5!	Kt–B3 [i]
20	Kt–K4!!	Resigns [j]

[*a*] In order to keep the Bishop's diagonal open.

[*b*] The famous "Stonewall" formation, which has crumbled more than once.

[*c*] The exchange has materially benefited White: his Knight is strongly posted at KB4, and Black is left with the "bad" Bishop (hemmed in by Black Pawns).

[*d*] A little trap: if 13 Q × P, Q–Kt5 regains the Pawn.

[*e*] The opening up of the game (signifying the smash-up of the "Stonewall") is in White's favor because he has more pieces in play.

[*f*] The more natural-looking 16 Kt × P could be answered by ... B–B4. If Black tries to parry the threat of 17 B × RP or 17 B × BP by playing 16 ... Q–Q3, then White wins with 17 B × RP!, Kt × B; 18 Kt–Kt6*ch*, K–Kt1; 19 Kt × R, Kt × Kt; 20 R–K8!, B–B4; 21 Q × B, R × R; 22 Q–B7*ch* etc.

[*g*] 17 ... B–B4? loses a piece.

[*h*] Prevents ... B–B4 and threatens R–KR5. White makes economical use of his superior development.

[*i*] Is everything protected?!

[*j*] For if 20 ... Kt × Kt; 21 Q × Kt wins (21 ... P–KR3; 22 Kt–Kt6*ch*, or 21 ... P–KKt3; 22 Kt × P*ch*). If 20 ... Q–K2; 21 Kt–Kt6*ch* wins the Queen. If 20 ... Q–B2; 21 Kt × Kt, P × Kt; 22 Kt–Kt6*ch* etc. All very neat and convincing.

TCHIGORIN'S HEIR

WHEN TCHIGORIN DIED in 1908, it seemed that the great Romantic tradition of attack in the grand manner had died with him. But this was not true: it will never be true so long as chess continues to be played. It did not take long before the chess world realized that Tchigorin had a worthy successor in young Rudolf Spielmann.

Like Tchigorin, Spielmann was well grounded in the theory of the game and equipped with first-rate technique in the endings; but, also like Tchigorin, he preferred the attack at all times, seasonable or unseasonable. And like Tchigorin, Spielmann left us a memorable treasure of beautiful, combinative chess.

FRENCH DEFENSE
Vienna, 1926

[After 11 ... O-O?]

	WHITE	BLACK
	R. Spielmann	R. Wahle
1	P–K4	P–K3
2	P–Q4	P–Q4
3	Kt–QB3	Kt–KB3
4	P×P	P×P
5	B–Kt5	B–K2
6	B–Q3	Kt–B3
7	KKt–K2	Kt–QKt5
8	Kt–Kt3	Kt×B*ch*
9	Q×Kt [a]	P–KKt3? [b]
10	O–O	P–B3
11	QR–K1	O–O? [c]*
12	R×B!!	Q×R [d]
13	Q–B3	K–Kt2 [e]

14	QKt–K4!!	P×Kt [f]
15	Kt×P	Q–K3 [g]
16	B×Kt*ch*	K–Kt1 [h]
17	Q–B4	*Resigns* [i]

[*a*] Tarrasch once made the jocular remark: "Without the King's Bishop I am like Rousseau without his cat." Spielmann needed no mascots.

[*b*] He wants to prevent Kt–B5, but this is too ambitious a plan. True, the weakness he has just created on his black squares is guarded by his King's Bishop; but, as Spielmann demonstrates with his usual tactical skill, this is an obstacle which can be removed without too much trouble.
Much better was 9 ... O–O followed by 10 ... P–KR3.

[*c*] 11 ... B–K3 was preferable, although in that case the advance P–B4–5 would leave Black in desperate straits. The text is a decisive blunder; but how many players could prove it?!

[*d*] The guardian Bishop is gone, and Black's fateful weakness on the black squares is opened up to a pin which leaves Black helpless.

[*e*] At first sight 13 ... B–B4 seems better. But after 14 Kt×B, P×Kt; 15 Q–Kt3!!, K–Kt2 (if 15 ... P–B5 or 15 ... K–R1; 16 Q–R4 wins); 16 B×Kt*ch!*, K×B; 17 Q–R4*ch*, K–K3; 18 R–K1*ch* Black can resign!

[*f*] Naturally forced.

[*g*] Or 15 ... Q×Kt; 16 Q×Kt*ch*, K–Kt1; 17 B–R6 and Black's defense caves in.

[*h*] If 16 ... K–R3; 17 Q–B4*ch* leads to mate.

[*i*] He is defenseless against 18 Q–R6. A little gem of a game.

COLLE

EDGARD COLLE WAS ONE of those romantics, like Marshall, Janowski and Spielmann, who live only for the attack. It was characteristic of his fiery play that he took one of the most harmless opening variations and made of it a fearsome weapon.

The game which follows is not an example of the Colle Variation, but it has remarkable points: playing the Black pieces, Colle crushes a future World Champion in 19 moves!

NIMZOINDIAN
DEFENSE

Amsterdam, 1926

[After 15 ... B × P!!]

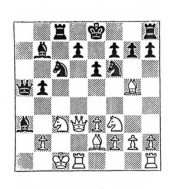

WHITE	BLACK
Dr. M. Euwe	*E. Colle*

	WHITE	BLACK
1	P–Q4	Kt–KB3
2	P–QB4	P–K3
3	Kt–QB3	B–Kt5
4	Q–B2	P–B4
5	Kt–B3	Kt–B3
6	P×P	B×P
7	B–Kt5	B–K2
8	O–O–O	Q–R4
9	P–QR3 [a]	P–QR3
10	P–K3	P–QKt3
11	B–K2	B–Kt2
12	Kt–QKt1 [b]	P–QKt4!
13	P×P [c]	P×P
14	Q–Q3 [d]	QR–B1!
15	Kt–B3	B×P!!*
16	B×Kt [e]	P×B [f]
17	K–Kt1	B×P!! [g]
18	Kt–R2 [h]	Kt–K4!
19	Kt×Kt [i]	B–Q4!
	Resigns	

[82]

[a] By castling Queen-side, White saves a tempo for doubling the Rooks on the Queen file in order to concentrate on Black's weak QP. However, White's King is anything but secure at QB1, as Colle's energetic play will demonstrate. In addition, White's last move has created a new target for Colle's attack.

[b] In order to threaten P–QKt4. But 12 R–Q2 followed ·by 13 KR–Q1 was more logical.

[c] White hopes to get good counterplay from the acceptance of the Pawn sacrifice involved in Colle's last move.

[d] Attacking the QKtP and also threatening to win a piece by 15 B×Kt and 16 Q×P*ch*. But Black gains precious time by threatening a killing discovered check.

[e] If 16 P×B, Kt–K4! or 16 Q×P, Q×Kt*ch*; 17 K–Kt1, Q–Kt5! and wins.

[f] He does not fear 17 Q×P*ch*, for after 17 ... K–B1; 18 Q×B??, Q×Kt*ch* forces mate!

[g] Beautiful! If now 18 K×B, Q–Kt5*ch*; 19 K–B2, Kt–K4!; 20 Kt×Kt, B–K5! winning.

[h] 18 Q×P*ch* holds out longer but leaves White with a lost game: 18 ... K–B1; 19 K×B (19 Q×B?, Q–R8*ch* leads to mate), Q–Kt5*ch*; 20 K–B2, Kt–K4; 21 Q–Q6*ch*, Q×Q; 22 R×Q, P–Kt5; 23 Kt×Kt, BP×Kt etc.

[i] If 19 Q×P, B–K5*ch*!; 20 K×B, R–B7*ch* etc. or 19 Q--Kt3, B–K5*ch*!; 20 K×B, R–B7*ch*; 21 K–R1, R×B and wins.

FROM ORTHODOX TO
UNORTHODOX

THE ORTHODOX DEFENSE to the Queen's Gambit is famous for its solidity and staying power. Yet one must not pore over the book variations excessively, for "the letter killeth." An unusual twist in White's play befuddles his opponent so badly that a slashing finish winds up the game in only 15 moves!

QUEEN'S GAMBIT
DECLINED

New York, 1926

WHITE	BLACK
Ed. Lasker	*B. Winkelman*

[After 14 ... Kt × Kt]

	WHITE	BLACK			
1	Kt–KB3	Kt–KB3			
2	P–Q4	P–Q4			
3	P–B4	P–K3			
4	B–Kt5	QKt–Q2			
5	P–K3	B–K2			
6	Kt–B3	O–O			
7	B–Q3 [a]	P–QR3			
8	Kt–K5!?	P × P [b]	12	Q–B3! [d]	Kt–Kt3
9	Kt × QBP	P–QKt4?? [c]	13	Kt–K4!	KKt–Q4 [e]
10	Kt–R5!	P–B4	14	Kt × B ch	Kt × Kt*
11	Kt–B6	Q–KI	15	Kt–B6 ch!!	Resigns [f]

[*a*] A departure from the Orthodox Variation, which continues 7 R–B1, P–B3 and then branches off into a number of lines which have undergone microscopic analysis.

[*b*] Playable, although 8 ... P–B4 is the natural and logical reply.

[*c*] An inexactitude which is refuted in masterly style. 9 ... P–B4 was still in order.

[*d*] White's play is very energetic. He threatens to win a Rook with 13 Kt × B*ch*. Note that 12 ... B–Kt2 would now lose a piece.

[*e*] There was no defense. A piquant variation: 13 ... B–Kt2; 14 Kt × B*ch*, Q × Kt; 15 Kt × Kt*ch*, P × Kt; 16 Q–R5 and Black must resign. Of course, 13 ... Q × Kt?? loses the Queen.

[*f*] Bowing to the inevitable. If 15 ... P × Kt; 16 B × P*ch!*, K × B; 17 Q–R5*ch*, K–Kt1; 18 B × P, Kt–Kt3; 19 Q–R6 and mate next move. A miniature classic!

IMMORTAL THEME

WHEN ANDERSSEN SACRIFICED two Rooks, the Queen etc. against Kieseritzky, the finished product was described as "*the* immortal game." It would be more accurate to call it "*an* immortal game," for since that time there have been many claimants to the title. Not the least deserving is the following little gem, on which Canal may have lavished somewhat less than five minutes. The game has the blazing quality of a Liszt improvisation.

CENTER COUNTER GAME

(Simultaneous Exhibition)

[After 10 ... O–O–O?]

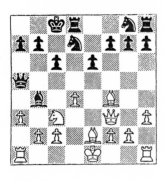

WHITE	BLACK
E. Canal	Amateur

	WHITE	BLACK		WHITE	BLACK
1	P–K4	P–Q4			
2	P×P	Q×P			
3	Kt–QB3	Q–QR4			
4	P–Q4	P–QB3 [a]			
5	Kt–B3	B–Kt5			
6	B–KB4	P–K3			
7	P–KR3	B×Kt? [b]			
8	Q×B	B–Kt5?			
9	B–K2	Kt–Q2	12	K–Q2	Q×R [d]
10	P–R3!	O–O–O? [c]*	13	Q×Pch!!	P×Q
11	P×B!!	Q×Rch	14	B–R6 mate	

[a] Superfluous. Development (4 ... Kt–KB3) is more to the point.

[b] Develops White's game. Better 7 ... B–KB4.

[c] The final blunder. His reliance on the pin receives a cruel jolt.

[d] Microscopically preferable was 12 ... Kt–K4; 13 B×Kt, Q×R; 14 Q×P, R–Q2 (amusing would be 14 ... Kt–K2; 15 Q×P*ch*, R–Q2; 16 B–Kt4, R–Q1; 17 Q–Q6*!* forcing mate); 15 Q–K8*ch*, R–Q1; 16 Q×KP*ch*, R–Q2; 17 Q–K8*ch*, R–Q1; 18 B–Kt4 *mate!*

TIME IS OF THE ESSENCE

I N ALMOST ALL VARIATIONS of the Nimzoindian Defense, time is of the essence. White generally acquires two Bishops against a Bishop and Knight, so that if the game is of the positional, slow-burning type, he generally comes off victorious. On the other hand, Black often has an early lead in development, and there are occasional opportunities for harrying the White Queen. Given the combination of hair-thin accurate timing by Black, and a careless move or two by White, we get a game like the following:

NIMZOINDIAN
DEFENSE

London, 1927

WHITE	BLACK
Sir G. A.	*W.*
Thomas	*Winter*

[After 10 P × P?]

	WHITE	BLACK
1	P–Q4	Kt–KB3
2	P–QB4	P–K3
3	Kt–QB3	B–Kt5
4	Q–B2	P–B4
5	P×P	Kt–R3 [a]
6	P–QR3	B×Kt*ch*
7	Q×B	Kt×P
8	P–QKt4 [b]	QKt–K5
9	Q–Q3	P–Q4!
10	P×P? [c]*	Kt×BP! [d]
11	K×Kt	Kt–Kt5*ch*
12	K–Kt3 [e]	Q–B3
13	Kt–B3 [f]	Q×R
14	B–Q2	Kt–B3
15	P–K4	P×P
16	P×P	O–O
17	B–B3?? [g]	Q×QB
	Resigns [h]	

[88]

[*a*] Black must now yield the Bishop-pair, else this Knight will be stranded at the side of the board.

[*b*] Attractive but premature; best is Rubinstein's 8 P–B3, keeping Black's Knights out of K5.

[*c*] 10 P–B3 was absolutely essential.

[*d*] Despite Black's lead in development, this interesting sacrifice comes as a surprise.

[*e*] If 12 K–K1, Q–B3 wins easily.

[*f*] The crucial variation was 13 K×Kt, P–R4*ch!*; 14 K–Kt3, P–R5*ch*; 15 K–R3, P×P*ch*; 16 P–Kt4, Q×B *mate*—or 13 R–Kt1, Q–B7*ch*; 14 K×Kt, P–R4*ch*; 15 K–R3 (15 K–Kt5, Q–B3 *mate*), P×P*ch* etc.

[*g*] White was lost in any event, but this move considerably hastens the end.

[*h*] For if 18 Q×Q, Kt–K5*ch* and Black is a whole Rook ahead.

FORESIGHT

O NE OF THE MASTER'S QUALITIES which earn the amateur's awe is the expert's ability to see ahead several moves. As a rule, the possibility of seeing ahead is determined by the nature of the position. Combinative situations, in which the opponent's moves can be forced and hence foreseen, are the ones in which calculation is easiest. Endgame positions, because of their simplified character, likewise lend themselves to precise calculation.

But aside from the nature of the position, there is another factor which affects calculation: the playing style of one's opponent. Nimzovich's moves were often so unorthodox that they could not be comprehended, much less foreseen.

SICILIAN DEFENSE

Kecskemet, 1927

*[After 14 ... Kt–Kt5]

	WHITE	BLACK
	A. Nimzovich	K. Gilg
1	P–K4	P–QB4
2	Kt–KB3	Kt–QB3
3	B–Kt5 [a]	Q–B2
4	P–B3	P–QR3
5	B–R4	Kt–B3
6	Q–K2	P–K4 [b]
7	O–O	B–K2
8	P–Q4! [c]	BP × P
9	P × P	Kt × QP
10	Kt × Kt	P × Kt
11	P–K5!	P–Q6 [d]
12	Q–K3!	Kt–Q4 [e]
13	Q–Kt3	P–KKt3 [f]
14	B–Kt3!	Kt–Kt5 [g]*

15	B × Pch! [h]	K–Q1 [i]
16	B–R6! [j]	Kt–B7
17	Kt–B3	Kt–Q5 [k]
18	Q × QP	Q × P
19	KR–K1	Q–B3
20	R × B!	Resigns [l]

[90]

[*a*] The first surprise: for most players, 3 P–Q4 is almost a religious rite.

[*b*] In order to prevent P–Q4.

[*c*] The second surprise: a powerful Pawn sacrifice.

[*d*] If 11 ... Kt–Q4; 12 P–K6, P×P; 13 Q×KP yields a strong attack.

[*e*] Or 12 ... B–B4; 13 Q–Kt3, Kt–K5; 14 Q×KtP, B×P*ch*; 15 K–R1*!* (if 15 R×B, Q×B*ch*), R–B1; 16 B–R6 and wins.

[*f*] If 13 ... O–O; 14 B–R6 wins the exchange.

[*g*] If 14 ... Q–B3; 15 Q–B3*!* is decisive.

[*h*] The third surprise: on 15 ... K×B; 16 P–K6*ch* wins the Queen.

[*i*] Black threatens ... Kt–B7 now.

[*j*] The fourth surprise: he laughs at the threat!

[*k*] On again, off again . . . if he snatches the Rook, there follows 18 Kt–Q5, Q–B3; 19 B–K3*!*, P–Q3 (or 19 ... B–B4; 20 Q–Kt5*ch*); 20 B–Kt6*ch*, K–Q2; 21 P–K6 *mate!*

[*l*] There is no good reply to the fifth and last surprise. If 20 ... K×R; 21 Kt–Q5*ch* forks the Queen. If 20 ... Q×R; 21 Q×Kt threatening 22 Q–Kt6 *mate* and also menacing the Black Rook.
And yet Nimzovich was fond of saying (doubtless with a twinkle in his eye) that he abhorred brutal play!

MOTHER GOOSE ON CHESS

M UCH HAS BEEN WRITTEN about the importance of Black's strategical aims in the Sicilian Defense. What is sometimes forgotten, however, is that it is an opening in which Black must guard with the greatest care against tactical surprises. Let his defensive measures slacken for a moment, and he will find himself in the sad position of the Three Wise Men of Gotham, who

"Went to sea in a bowl;
If the bowl had been stronger
My song had been longer."

SICILIAN DEFENSE
Amsterdam, 1929

[After 11 ... B × Kt]

WHITE	BLACK
H. Weenink	W. Schelfhout
1 P–K4	P–QB4
2 Kt–KB3	P–K3
3 P–Q4	P × P
4 Kt × P	Kt–KB3
5 Kt–QB3	B–Kt5 [a]
6 B–Q3	Kt–B3 [b]
7 Kt × Kt	KtP × Kt? [c]
8 P–K5	Kt–Q4
9 Q–Kt4!	P–Kt3 [d]
10 O–O! [e]	P–KB4? [f]
11 P × P e.p.	B × Kt [g]*

12 B × Pch!	K–B1 [h]
13 B–R6ch	K–Kt1
14 P–B7 mate [i]	

[*a*] An aggressive move, but also a dangerous one, as it leaves the King-side open to attack.

[*b*] Playable, although the safest course is 6 ... P–K4 followed by 7 ... P–Q4.
A game Treybal–Rejfir, Prague, 1933, went 6 ... P–Q4; 7 P–K5*!*, KKt–Q2; 8 Q–Kt4, B–B1 (Black seems quite safe); 9 Kt×KP*!*, Q–R4; 10 Kt×P*ch*, K–Q1; 11 B–Kt5*ch*, *resigns*!

[*c*] Much better is 7 ... QP×Kt, so that if 8 P–K5, Kt–Q2; 9 Q–Kt4*?*, Q–R4*!*

[*d*] The pin is worthless to Black, as 9 ... Kt×Kt*?* would be very poor play.

[*e*] Black has a difficult choice before him: White threatens to win a piece with 11 Kt×Kt. Neither 10 ... Kt×Kt; 11 Q×B*!* nor 10 ... B×Kt; 11 P×B (followed by B–R3) is satisfactory for him.

[*f*] Trying to temporize, he makes matters still worse.

[*g*] Or 11 ... Q×P; 12 Kt×Kt winning a piece. But the trouble with the text is that White need not play the expected 12 P×B.

[*h*] If 12 ... P×B; 13 Q×Kt*Pch*, K–B1; 14 Q–Kt7*ch*, K–K1; 15 P–B7*ch*, K–K2; 16 P–B8(Q) *mate* (*both* Queens are *en prise*!).

[*i*] This is what comes of not reading Mother Goose!

GRAND ILLUSION

WHEN WE PLAY over Capablanca's games, we are irresistibly reminded of Morphy. Both had Spanish blood, both learned the moves at an early age, both were child prodigies, both journeyed from the New World to the Old in search of glory.

A first-rate Capablanca game gives us the feeling that chess is a very easy game indeed: his finest victories seem simple, lucid, inevitable. It is a delusion, but a delicious one. Champions, like other mortals, yearn for the secret of eternal youth; and before every champion there stands the specter of eventual decline and dethronement.

NIMZOINDIAN DEFENSE

Carlsbad, 1929

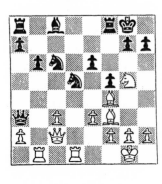

*[After 16 B–B3!!]

WHITE	BLACK
J. R.	*H.*
Capablanca	*Mattison*

	WHITE	BLACK
1	P–Q4	Kt–KB3
2	P–QB4	P–K3
3	Kt–QB3	B–Kt5
4	Q–B2	P–B4
5	P×P	Kt–B3
6	Kt–B3	B×P
7	B–B4	P–Q4
8	P–K3	Q–R4?
9	B–K2	B–Kt5
10	O–O	B×Kt
11	P×B	O–O [a]
12	QR–Kt1!	Q–R6
13	KR–Q1!	P–QKt3
14	P×P	Kt×P [b]
15	Kt–Kt5!	P–B4
16	B–B3!!*	Q–B4 [c]
17	P–B4!! [d]	Kt(4)–Kt5
18	Q–Kt3	P–K4 [e]
19	P–QR3!!	Kt–R3 [f]
20	B×Kt	*Resigns* [g]

[*a*] Black has played the opening poorly. His Queen is out of the game and exposed to attack; his deserted King-side is inadequately defended. The exchange of Bishop for Knight has left White with two Bishops, open lines and a clear initiative.

[*b*] If 14 ... P×P; 15 P–B4! is very strong (15 ... P×P; 16 B–Q6 etc.).

[*c*] This stops 17 R×Kt, but has no further value. Yet, as will be seen from the following variations, Black is at the mercy of the omnipotent Bishops.
The chief threat is of course 17 R×Kt. On 16 ... Kt(3)–K2; 17 P–B4 wins the exchange, while if 16 ... Kt(4)–K2?; 17 B–Q6 wins at least a piece. 16 ... Kt× B?; 17 B×Kt also costs Black a piece. 16 ... R–Q1 is of no avail, being refuted by 17 P–B4, Kt(4)–Kt5; 18 R×Kt, R×R*ch*; 19 Q×R, Q×R; 20 B×Kt etc. What defenses remain? If 16 ... Q×BP?; 17 Q×Q, Kt×Q; 18 B×Kt with an overwhelming material advantage. Finally, if 16 ... P–KR3; 17 R×Kt!, P×Kt; 18 B–Q6, Q–R3; 19 B×R, P×R; 20 B×P*ch*, K×B; 21 B×Kt, R–Kt1; 22 Q–Q2!, K–K2; 23 R–Q1 and wins.

[*d*] The threat is of course not 18 P×Kt??, but 18 R–Kt5! winning a piece. In the event of 17 ... Kt–B3 or 17 ... R–Q1; 18 R–Kt5 still wins a piece. Even more elegant is 17 ... Kt×B; 18 R–Kt5!, Q–K2; 19 B×Kt, Q×Kt; 20 P×Kt! and it is all over.

[*e*] Something must be done about the devastating threat of 19 B–Q6.

[*f*] Or 19 ... P×B; 20 P×Kt winning a piece.

[*g*] For if 20 ... Q×B; 21 P–B5*ch*, K–R1; 22 Kt–B7*ch*, K–Kt1; 23 Kt–R6*ch*, K–R1; 24 Q–Kt8*ch*! etc. An exquisite game.

TIME MARCHES ON

ONE EVENING, A GOOD MANY YEARS AGO, I was very much taken with a pretty little game played in a Metropolitan League match. "Here," I said to myself, "is the perfect refutation of the view that modern chess is dull. This game deserves to be published!" I clipped the score out of a newspaper and carefully placed the clipping in my wallet. Many a time I was on the point of annotating and publishing the game, but always something intervened. My wallets wore out, I bought new ones, but the clipping, like its contents, was indestructible.

At last the time has come to publish the game. Alas, almost two decades have passed since it was played! Can it still be called modern?!

QUEEN'S GAMBIT DECLINED

New York, 1929

[After 14 ... P × B?]

WHITE	BLACK
M. Hanauer	F. Bartha

	WHITE	BLACK
1	P–Q4	Kt–KB3
2	Kt–KB3	P–K3
3	P–B4	P–Q4
4	B–Kt5	QKt–Q2
5	P–K3	B–K2
6	QKt–Q2 [a]	O–O
7	B–Q3	P–QR3 [b]
8	O–O	P–B4
9	Q–K2	R–K1 [c]
10	KR–Q1	BP×P
11	KP×P	P×P [d]
12	Kt×P	P–QKt4
13	Kt(4)–K5	B–Kt2

	WHITE	BLACK
14	B × Kt	P × B? [e]*
15	Kt × P!!	K × Kt
16	Kt–K5ch!!	P × Kt [f]
17	Q–R5ch	K–Kt2
18	Q × RPch	K–B1
19	Q–R6ch	K–Kt1
20	B–R7ch	Resigns [g]

[96]

[a] Capablanca's idea: he intends to answer an eventual ... P ✕ P with Kt ✕ P, bringing this piece into powerful play at K5.

[b] The simplest course, and quite good for equalizing purposes, is ... P–B4 followed by ... P–QKt3, ... B–Kt2 etc.

[c] Weakening the King Bishop's Pawn, without any apparent purpose.

[d] He lets the Knight come into play because he is intent on burdening White with an isolated Pawn.

[e] Played with a laudable objective: keeping White's Knights out of K5. But now White has a winning attack.

[f] King moves transpose into the text continuation. 16 ... Kt ✕ Kt; 17 Q–R5ch wins easily for White.

[g] If 20 ... K–R1 White mates in three. If 20 ... K–B2 White mates in two. Note that White could have forced an immediate mate with 19 B–Kt6!

CREATING COMPLICATIONS

THROUGHOUT THIS GAME, White plays for complications in order to make life hard for his opponent. Such a course naturally carries a certain amount of risk, but in practical play the advantage is almost invariably with the attacker. The mood of the aggressor is buoyant, optimistic and often inspired; the defender, in all too many cases, is easily intimidated, fatigued or bored.

TWO KNIGHTS' DEFENSE

Paris, 1929

WHITE	BLACK
I.	*V.*
Gudju	*Bogdanovsky*
1 P–K4	P–K4
2 Kt–KB3	Kt–QB3
3 B–B4	Kt–B3
4 P–Q4	P×P
5 O–O	Kt×P
6 R–K1	P–Q4
7 Kt–B3!?	B–K3 [a]
8 Kt×Kt	P×B
9 QKt–Kt5	Q–Q4 [b]
10 Kt×BP!	K×Kt
11 Kt–Kt5ch	K–Kt1
12 Kt×B	R–B1 [c]

*[After 19 Q–Kt4ch!!]

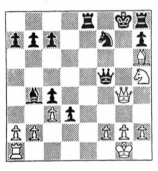

13 B–R6!?	B–Kt5 [d]
14 Kt×KtP!?	Kt–K4 [e]
15 R–K2	P–Q6 [f]
16 P–QB3	Kt–B2 [g]
17 Kt–R5!	Q–KB4 [h]
18 R–K8ch!!	R×R
19 Q–Kt4ch!!	Resigns [i]*

[98]

[*a*] White's last move is puzzling. A game Kendall–Borochow (Correspondence, 1935) continued 7 ... P×B; 8 R×Kt*ch*, B–K3; 9 Kt×P, Kt×Kt; 10 R×Kt, Q–K2; 11 Kt–K4, R–Q1; 12 B–Kt5, P–KB3?; 13 R×R*ch*, Q×R; 14 Kt×P*ch*, *resigns.*

[*b*] Leads to trouble. 9 ... B–K2 is safer.

[*c*] 12 ... B–Q3 looks more promising.

[*d*] If 13 ... P×B; 14 Q–Kt4*ch*, K–B2; 15 R–K4*!* (with the subtle threat 16 Q–B3*ch*, K–Kt1; 17 R–Kt4 *ch*), Kt–K2; 16 QR–K1 and Black's game is untenable. 13 ... B–Kt5 is hard to understand, as White can simply play 14 P–QB3.

[*e*] Could he have taken the Rook? Apparently not: 14 ... B×R; 15 Q–Kt4, B×P*ch* (if 15 ... K–B2; 16 R×B with a decisive attack); 16 K×B, R–B1*ch*; 17 Kt–B5*ch*, K–B2; 18 B×R, R×B; 19 Q–Kt7*ch* and wins.

[*f*] 15 ... Kt–B2 would be answered as in the game. If 15 ... B–B1; 16 Kt–R5*!*, Q–K3; 17 R×Kt*!*

[*g*] Seems to win material.

[*h*] This has all the earmarks of a crushing rejoinder: three White pieces are *en prise*! (Of course, not 17 ... Q×Kt; 18 R–K8*ch*.) With the nonchalance of a film hero, White now concludes in superb style.

[*i*] If 19 ... Q×Q; 20 Kt–B6 *mate.*

SQUEEZE PLAY

IT USUALLY REQUIRES anywhere from 30 to 40 moves to
achieve the paralyzing positional bind so dear to the heart
of the modern master. Rare indeed is a game like the
following one, in which a player is reduced to complete move-
starvation in 20 moves! Even more remarkable is the fact that
Black is not the victim of brilliant sacrificial play. White's
moves are quiet, but they speak volumes.

QUEEN'S GAMBIT DECLINED

Rotterdam, 1929

[After 20 B–Kt5!]

	WHITE	BLACK
	S. Landau	Ten Kate
1	P–Q4	P–Q4
2	P–QB4	P–QB3
3	Kt–KB3	Kt–B3
4	Kt–B3	P–K3
5	B–Kt5	B–K2
6	P–K3	QKt–Q2
7	R–B1	O–O
8	B–Q3 [a]	P–QKt3 [b]
9	P×P	Kt×P? [c]
10	Kt×Kt	BP×Kt [d]
11	B×B	Q×B
12	R–B7!	Q–Kt5ch? [e]
13	Q–Q2	Q×Qch
14	K×Q	P–QR3 [f]
15	KR–QB1	R–Q1
16	R(1)–B6	P–R3
17	R–Q6	K–B1
18	Kt–K5 [g]	K–K1 [h]
19	Kt–B6	P–QR4 [i]
20	B–Kt5!*	Resigns [j]

[100]

[a] So far the game has been ultra-Orthodox; but now, instead of the regulation 8 ... P×P; 9 B×P, Kt-Q4 there follows a weak move which leads to trouble.

[b] Unless Black is very careful, he may find himself burdened with a weakness on the Queen's Bishop file.

[c] Not good, as it opens up the file for White's powerfully posted Rook. 9 ... KP×P should have been tried.

[d] If 10 ... B×B; 11 Kt-Kt4, P-QB4; 12 B-K4 winning the exchange.

[e] Black finds his opponent's grip on the open file extremely irksome. He should therefore have tried 12 ... Q-Q3, for if 13 Q-B2, Kt-B4!

[f] Simplification has brought no relief. If 14 ... Kt-B3; 15 Kt-K5 and the Bishop has no exit for development.

[g] Tighter and tighter: the bind proceeds apace.

[h] Or 18 ... K-K2; 19 R×P and Black's situation is hopeless.

[i] If 19 ... P-QKt4 (what else?); 20 P-QKt4 and Black is strangled.

[j] Any move with a piece will cost Black at least a piece. He can stave off the catastrophe with Pawn moves for a while, but the loss of at least a piece is inevitable. (Chernev indicates the possibility 20 ... B-R3; 21 B×B, R×B; 22 R[6]×Kt!, R×R; 23 R-B8ch, R-Q1; 24 R×R mate!) A position that Nimzovich would have been proud of!

THE DRAGON STRIKES BACK

MANY ATTEMPTS HAVE BEEN MADE to slay the Sicilian Dragon: some have succeeded, others have failed. Despite the most intensive study and practice, the last word still remains to be said. The opening manuals generally incline in White's favor, yet in actual play Black makes a satisfactory showing. The practical results therefore bespeak a hard inner core of resistance which promises well for the durability of the "Dragon."

In common with other defenses which are somewhat cramping but resilient, the Dragon Variation is a line of play in which Black, given favorable conditions, can strike back with all the breathtaking thrust of an uncoiled spring.

SICILIAN DEFENSE

Budapest, 1933

*[After 16 Kt–K2?]

	WHITE	BLACK
	G. Meszaros	I. Wessel
1	P–K4	P–QB4
2	Kt–KB3	Kt–QB3
3	P–Q4	P×P
4	Kt×P	Kt–B3
5	Kt–QB3	P–Q3
6	B–K2	P–KKt3
7	O–O	B–Kt2
8	B–K3	O–O
9	Kt–Kt3	P–QR3 [a]
10	P–QR4 [b]	B–K3
11	Kt–Q4 [c]	Kt×Kt
12	B×Kt	Q–R4
13	P–B4	QR–B1 [d]
14	B–B3	R–B5
15	R–K1? [e]	Kt–Kt5!
16	Kt–K2? [f]*	R×B!!
17	Kt×R	Q×Rch!!
18	Q×Q	B×Ktch
19	K–R1 [g]	Kt–B7ch
	Resigns [h]	

[*a*] One of the most critical lines in the Dragon Variation is
9 ... B–K3; 10 P–B4, Kt–QR4; 11 P–B5, B–B5;
12 P–Kt4! when Black finds himself in difficulties.

[*b*] Rather pointless. 10 P–B4 and if 10 ... P–QKt4;
11 B–B3 is far more promising.

[*c*] A wandering Knight.

[*d*] Black has completed his development without any effort.

[*e*] This leads to trouble, but it was no longer easy to suggest
a good continuation.

[*f*] If 16 B×Kt (not 16 B×B?, Q–B4*ch* and wins), Black
wins easily with 16 ... B×B*ch*; 17 K–R1, B×B;
18 Q×B, B×Kt etc. or 16 ... R×B; 17 Q–B3,
B×B; 18 Q×B, R–Q7 etc.
The move White actually chooses is still worse!

[*g*] Now the light dawns. On 19 K–B1, B–B5*ch* White
must reply 20 Q–K2 (20 B–K2??, Kt×P *mate!*),
B×Q*ch* and Black has won a piece.

[*h*] 20 K–Kt1, Kt–Q6*ch* leaves White a piece down.

PLANLESSNESS

O NE OF THE GREAT LESSONS of modern master play is that purely passive policy has little chance of success when one's opponent has greater command of the board. The reason generally given is the impressive development in the ability to exploit crowded positions.

But the question is not merely one of technique. How does a player get a bad position? He plays a poor opening whose potentialities he does not foresee; he fails to plan creatively for the future; he does not offer the best resistance in the ensuing difficult position. Then comes one tactical explosion, and it is all over.

QUEEN'S GAMBIT
DECLINED

Ujpest, 1934

*[After 14 ... Kt–B5?]

	WHITE	BLACK
	P. Frydman	Dr. M. Vidmar
1	P–Q4	P–Q4
2	Kt–KB3	Kt–KB3
3	P–B4	P–B3
4	P×P	P×P
5	Kt–B3	Kt–B3
6	B–B4	P–K3
7	P–K3	B–K2 [a]
8	B–Q3	O–O
9	O–O	P–QR3 [b]
10	R–B1!	B–Q2 [c]
11	Kt–K5	R–B1
12	P–QR3	Kt–QR4 [d]
13	Q–B3	P–QKt4

14	Q–R3! [e]	Kt–B5?*
15	Kt×QP!!	P–Kt3 [f]
16	Kt×Bch	Q×Kt [g]
17	B×Kt!	R×B [h]
18	R×R!	P×R
19	B–Kt5!	Resigns [i]

[*a*] The simplifying exchange on the fourth move is a bit deceptive, as the variation harbors a good deal of venom behind its sedate appearance. Black should have sought more simplification with 7 ... B–Q3.

[*b*] And here Emanuel Lasker's 9 ... Kt–KR4 is preferable.

[*c*] Renouncing 10 ... P–QKt4 because of 11 Kt×KtP*!*, P×Kt; 12 R×Kt, R×P; 13 Q–Kt3*!* winning a Pawn.

[*d*] Black's position is none too promising. He initiates a Queen-side offensive, but meanwhile White builds up a formidable attack on the other wing.

[*e*] With a veiled threat which Black should have parried by 14 ... P–Kt3; although after 15 B–R6, R–K1; 16 P–B4 White would have a formidable attack.

[*f*] Nothing left but chagrin. If 15 ... P×Kt (not 15 ... KKt×Kt*??*; 16 Q×P *mate*); 16 Kt×B winning at least the exchange: 17 Kt×Kt*ch* is threatened, and Black cannot play 16 ... Q×Kt (again, if 16 ... Kt×Kt*??*; 17 Q×P *mate*); 17 B×P*ch*, K–R1; 18 B–B5*ch* etc.
And 15 ... P–R3 is refuted by 16 Kt×Kt*ch*, B×Kt; 17 B×RP, P×B; 18 Q×RP etc.

[*g*] There are many ways to win now, but White chooses the quickest.

[*h*] A despairing offer of the exchange; White ignores it!

[*i*] Quite right: he cannot meet the triple threat of 20 Kt–Kt4, 20 Kt×B and 20 B×Kt.

FLOHR

ALO FLOHR HAS THE REPUTATION of favoring the quiet by-paths of position play. When he is in the mood, however, he reveals himself as an able tactician with a sharp sense of timing. This is a particularly useful asset in the following game, in which each player stages his attack on a different wing.

ENGLISH OPENING
Liebwerda, 1934

[After 14 ... P × B]

WHITE	BLACK
R. Pitschak	S. Flohr

1	P–QB4	P–K4	
2	Kt–QB3	Kt–KB3	
3	P–KKt3	P–Q4	
4	P × P	Kt × P	
5	B–Kt2	Kt–Kt3	
6	Kt–B3	Kt–B3	
7	O–O	B–K2	
8	P–Q3	O–O	
9	B–K3	B–KKt5	
10	P–KR3	B–R4 [a]	
11	R–B1	Q–Q2	
12	Kt–QR4	B × Kt	
13	B × B [b]	Q × RP	
14	B × Kt? [c]	P × B*	

15	R × P [d]	Kt–Q4! [e]
16	Q–K1 [f]	P–B4! [g]
17	B–B5	P–B5! [h]
18	B × B	P × P
19	P × P	Kt–K6
	Resigns [i]

[106]

[*a*] White is to take the initiative on the Queen-side, playing R–B1 followed by the occupation of QB5. Black's best course is counterplay on the other wing. Hence the aggressive development of his Queen's Bishop, which has provoked a weakening of White's King-side.

[*b*] Too timid: the unorthodox 13 P×B gives him an excellent game, for example 13 ... Kt×Kt (or 13 ... KR–Q1; 14 P–B4! and White's Bishops are very strong); 14 Q×Kt, Q×QP; 15 P–B4! recovering the Pawn with a good game.

[*c*] A second and this time grave mistake: the absence of this Bishop will cost White the game in short order. Better was 14 B–Kt2, Q–Q2; 15 KB×Kt, P×B; 16 K–Kt2 and White has positional compensation for his Pawn.

[*d*] If he plays 15 Kt×Kt (in order to prevent the later inroad by Black's Knight), RP×Kt; 16 R×P Black continues the attack with 16 ... B–Q3 followed by 17 ... P–B4 etc. (White must not play 17 B×P? because of 17 ... Q–Q2.)

[*e*] With the double threat of ... Kt×B and ... Kt–B3–Kt5.

[*f*] On 16 Q–Q2, Kt–B3 wins the exchange because of the threatened ... Kt–Kt5. Similarly, if 16 B–B5, B×B; 17 Kt×B, Kt–B3.

[*g*] If 16 ... Kt–B3; White has 17 P–B3.

[*h*] Flohr is in his element. This wins at once.

[*i*] A clever finish by Flohr. If 19 R–B2, Q×P*ch* wins.

8—(G.370)

FIRST COME, FIRST SERVED

C HESS, CONTRARY TO THE IMPRESSION held in some quarters, is not a game for timid souls. It is a contest which requires, and evokes, considerable combative vigor. Since it is not considered proper to smash the board and pieces over your opponent's head whenever you make a mistake, the pent-up energy must take the form of powerful attacking moves. Let either player falter or fail to recognize the coming of the crisis, and he will find himself the victim of a murderous onslaught (by his opponent's pieces, of course!).

QUEEN'S GAMBIT
DECLINED

Bad Lovisa, 1934

*[After 16 R × P!!?]

WHITE	BLACK
R. Krogius	I. Niemala
1 P–Q4	Kt–KB3
2 P–QB4	P–K3
3 B–Kt5	P–Q4
4 P–K3	QKt–Q2
5 Kt–KB3	B–K2
6 QKt–Q2 [a]	O–O
7 B–Q3	P–QKt3
8 Q–B2	B–Kt2
9 P×P	P×P [b]
10 Kt–K5	Kt×Kt!
11 P×Kt	Kt–K5! [c]
12 P–KR4!?	Kt×B [d]

13 P×Kt	P–Kt3
14 P–B4	P–QB4 [e]
15 Q–Q1	P–B5
16 R×P!!?*	P×B? [f]
17 K–B2!!	P–B3 [g]
18 Q–R1	Resigns [h]

[108]

[a] For another example of this somewhat unusual move, see Hanauer–Bartha, page 96.

[b] Black is now prepared to free his game a bit with ... P–B4. Therefore, instead of contenting himself with the routine 10 O–O, White tries to hold the initiative.

[c] He need not fear exchanges, for example: 12 B×B, Q×B; 13 Kt×Kt?, P×Kt and Black wins a Pawn (14 B×P??, Q–Kt5ch). Or 12 Kt×Kt, P×Kt; 13 B×B, Q×B with the same variation.

[d] The opening of the KR file is risky; the same is true of 12 ... B×B, with the possible continuation 13 P×B, Q×P; 14 Kt×Kt, Q×KtP?; 15 Kt–B6ch!, P×Kt; 16 O–O–O and wins!

[e] In order to drive White's Bishop off the strong attacking diagonal. 14 ... B×P; 15 P×B, Q×P brings in three Pawns for a piece, but White's attack continues unabated.

[f] White's last move had the impact of a solar plexus blow: if 16 ... K×R?; 17 Q–R5ch, K–Kt2; 18 Q–R6ch, K–Kt1; 19 B×KtP, P×B; 20 Q×Pch, K–R1; 21 K–B2! and wins.
But there *was* a defense: had Black not been demoralized, he would have played 16 ... B×P! (fighting back!); 17 B×KtP! (best), B–R5ch!; 18 K–B1, P×B; 19 R×QB, Q–B1; 20 Kt–B3, Q×R; 21 Kt×B with chances for both sides.

[g] Or 17 ... K×R; 18 Q–R1ch, K–Kt1; 19 Q–R6 and Black must helplessly await 20 R–R1. A curious line is 17 ... B×P; 18 Q–R1!, B–KB3; 19 Q–R6! and again 20 R–R1 decides.

[h] Against the threat of 19 Q–R6 he has only 18 ... R–B2, allowing 19 R–R8ch and mate next move. A brisk tragi-comedy of errors.

PURELY COINCIDENTAL

SOME TIME AGO I came across a very beautiful game played by Naidorf in the days when he was just beginning to make a name for himself. This gem, a veritable orgy of sacrifices, might be said to out-Anderssen Anderssen. Yet the game gave me a vague sense of disquiet: somewhere I had seen a game very much like it. A protracted search failed to produce the score I wanted. Finally, an astonishing discovery cleared up the mystery: there were two games, identical for the first twelve moves, both featuring the same initial surprise sacrifice! It is certain, however, that the *second* version was not based on knowledge of the *earlier* game. For Naidorf's game, which has priority, is incomparably more brilliant.

FRENCH DEFENSE

Riga, 1934

[After 12 ... Kt–B1]

WHITE	BLACK
A. Strautmanis	V. Hasenfuss
1 P–K4	P–K3
2 P–Q4	P–Q4
3 Kt–QB3	P×P [a]
4 Kt×P	Kt–Q2
5 Kt–KB3	KKt–B3
6 B–Q3	B–K2
7 O–O	P–QKt3 [b]
8 Kt–K5!	B–Kt2
9 Kt×Ktch	P×Kt? [c]
10 Kt×P!!	K×Kt
11 Q–R5ch	K–Kt1 [d]
12 R–K1	Kt–B1 [e]*
13 B–KR6 [f]	P–KB4
14 R–K3! [g]	Q–K1 [h]

15 R–Kt3ch	Kt–Kt3
16 B–QB4	B–KB1 [i]
17 Q×P!	B×B [j]
18 B×Pch	K–Kt2
19 Q–K5ch	K–B1
20 Q–B6ch	*Resigns* [k]

[110]

[*a*] This has a bad reputation: White gets too much freedom.

[*b*] From bad to worse. Castling is much safer.

[*c*] Loses by force! 9 ... B×Kt should have been played, although White's position would be distinctly superior.

[*d*] White's sacrifice is astonishing and beautiful: astonishing because sacrifices at KB7 are rare in close openings, beautiful because the sequel requires subtle timing. Note that 11 ... K–Kt2? or 11 ... K–B1? is bad because of 12 B–R6*ch* gaining valuable time.

[*e*] If 12 ... B–Q4; 13 P–QB4 etc. Or 12 ... Q–K1?; 13 Q–Kt4*ch* and Black can resign.

[*f*] Very strong, as it threatens 14 Q–Kt4*ch* with killing effect. An interesting alternative is 13 R×P*!!*, Kt×R; 14 B–QB4, Q–Q3; 15 B–KR6, B–KB1; 16 R–K1, B–B1 (if 16 ... B×B; 17 B×Kt*ch*, K–Kt2; 18 Q–B7 *mate*); 17 Q–K8*!*, B–Q2; 18 R×Kt*!!*, R×Q; 19 R×R*ch*, B–K3; 20 B×B*ch*, Q×B; 21 R×B *mate!* (Naidorf–Sapiro, Lodz, *1929*).

[*g*] Preparing to strengthen the pressure.

[*h*] He has nothing better, but now Chernev indicates a beautiful win with 15 Q×P*!!*, P×Q; 16 B–B4*ch*, Q–B2 (or 16 ... Kt–K3; 17 B×Kt*ch*, Q–B2; 18 R–Kt3*ch* and mate next move); 17 R×B*!!*, Q×B; 18 R–Kt7 *mate!*

[*i*] Or 16 ... B–Q4; 17 B×B, P×B; 18 R–K1, Q–B2; 19 R×B*!*, Q×R; 20 R×Kt*ch!* leading to mate.

[*j*] "Best" was 17 ... B–Q4; 18 KB×B, P×B; 19 Q×P*ch*, Q–B2; 20 Q×R with an easy win.

[*k*] What a pity that such a pretty game must be dismissed as second-rate!

TOO LATE OR TOO SOON?

A S THE INHERITOR of the Romantic tradition of attack,
Spielmann continued to play the King's Gambit long
after every other player of note had discarded it. In
the middle '20s he wrote an article entitled *From the Sickbed
of the King's Gambit*, and finally, in 1929 he took the long
overdue step of beginning to play the abhorrent 1 P–Q4.
With this move, he won many a pretty game—doubtless to his
astonishment.

Yet Spielmann's career ended on a note of tragic irony; for
since his death the younger masters have revived the King's
Gambit with marked success!

*QUEEN'S GAMBIT
DECLINED*

Sopron, 1934

[After 16 R–B3]

WHITE	BLACK
R. *Spielmann*	I. *Fuss*
1 P–Q4	Kt–KB3
2 Kt–KB3	P–K3
3 P–B4	B–Kt5*ch*
4 QKt–Q2	Kt–K5
5 P–K3	Kt×Kt
6 B×Kt	B×B*ch*
7 Q×B	P–Q4
8 R–B1	P–QB3
9 B–Q3	Kt–Q2
10 O–O	O–O
11 P–K4! [a]	P×KP
12 B×P	Kt–B3
13 B–Kt1	P–QKt3

14 Q–B4	B–Kt2
15 Kt–K5	Q–B2? [b]
16 R–B3 [c]*	Kt–R4 [d]
17 B×P*ch!*	K×B [e]
18 R–KR3	K–Kt1 [f]
19 R×Kt	P–B3 [g]
20 R–R8*ch!*	*Resigns* [h]

[112]

[*a*] By a roundabout route the game has transposed into the semi-Slav Defense. True to his style, Spielmann opens up the game at the first opportunity.

[*b*] A triple blunder: (*a*) he removes the Queen from the menaced King-side; (*b*) he exposes his Queen to a discovered attack; (*c*) he leaves his Bishop bottled up.
15 ... P–B4 followed in due course by ... Q–K2 would have set White far more difficult problems.

[*c*] "Suddenly" White has a terrific attack!

[*d*] If instead 16 ... P–B4; 17 R–KKt3, K–R1 (17 ... Kt–Q2 or 17 ... Kt–K1 is refuted by 18 B×P*ch!* while if 17 ... Kt–R4; 18 Q–R6*!*); 18 Kt–Kt6*ch* winning the Queen!
If Black guards the Queen with 16 ... QR–B1 then 17 R–KKt3, K–R1 (or 17 ... Kt–R4; 18 Q–R6*!*); 18 R×P*!!*, K×R; 19 Q–Kt5*ch*, K–R1; 20 Q×Kt*ch*, K–Kt1; 21 R–K1*!*, KR–Q1 (or 21 ... Q–Q1; 22 Q–R6, P–KB4; 23 R–K3 winning); 22 B×P*ch!*, K–B1 (if 22 ... K×B; 23 R–K3 leads to mate); 23 Kt–Kt6*ch*, K–K1; 24 R×P*ch!* forcing mate very nicely.

[*e*] Forced (17 ... K–R1; 18 Kt–Kt6*ch*).

[*f*] The only way to hold on (precariously!) was 18 ... P–Kt3; 19 Kt×KtP*!* leaving White two Pawns ahead.

[*g*] If 19 ... Q–K2 (to stop 20 Q–R4); 20 Q–Kt4 followed by 21 Q–R3 ends it all.

[*h*] If 20 ... K×R; 21 Kt–Kt6*ch* wins the Queen. A typically incisive Spielmann attack.

RIDDLE

IT IS SOMETHING of a psychological riddle when an aggressive player like Keres adopts the French Defense, which has the reputation of being conservative. But the riddle is easily explained. As we have seen, this defense is a standing invitation to adventurous spirits to indulge in premature attacks —while lazy optimists are tempted to play second-rate moves.

Against a player of Keres' brilliant stamp, sleazy opening play is likely to recoil with savage effect.

FRENCH DEFENSE

Correspondence, 1935

WHITE	BLACK
G. Menke	*P. Keres*
1 P–K4	P–K3
2 P–Q4	P–Q4
3 Kt–QB3	Kt–KB3
4 P–K5	KKt–Q2
5 Kt–B3?	P–QB4
6 P×P	B×P
7 B–QKt5?	P–QR3
8 B×Kt*ch*	Kt×B [*a*]
9 O–O	P–QKt4
10 P–QR3	B–Kt2 [*b*]
11 B–B4	P–Q5! [*c*]*

[After 11 ... P–Q5!]

12 Kt–R2 [*d*]	KR–Kt1!!
13 Kt×P [*e*]	Q–R5!
14 Kt–K2 [*f*]	P–Kt4!
	Resigns [*g*]

[a] White's insipid play has yielded Keres an easy initiative.

[b] "Castle when you have to," said the great Pillsbury, "or when you want to." The ability to be discriminating about when to castle, shows the hand of a master. It will soon be clear that Keres' avoidance of castling is intentional.

[c] Offering a Pawn to open up the long diagonal.

[d] A miserable square for the Knight; but if 12 Kt×QP, Q–R5; 13 P–KKt3 (or 13 B–K3, Kt×P with a beautiful game for Black), Q–R6; 14 P–B3, P–Kt4!; 15 B×P, Kt×P; 16 B–B6, Kt–Kt5 and wins.

[e] Now we see why Black avoided castling. His threat was 13 ... P–Kt4; 14 B–Kt3, P–KR4 forcing a file open on the King-side.

[f] Too bad; Keres had anticipated 14 P–KKt3, P–Kt4!!; 15 B–K3 (capturing the Queen leads to mate!), Q–K5 and wins!

[g] Bishop moves are decisively answered by 15 ... Q–K5! An original game all the way.

8,372,849,743 TIMES 6,247,623,822

WHEN PROFESSOR WEINER of the Massachusetts Institute of Technology invented a calculating machine which requires only one ten-thousandth of a second for the most complicated computations, he was quoted as saying, "I defy you to describe a capacity of the human brain which I cannot duplicate with electronic devices."

Up to the time these lines were written, the Professor had apparently not yet perfected an electronic device capable of making such chess moves as Tartakover's 20th in the following game. The day may yet come, however, when we shall see such books as "Robot's 1000 Best Games," or when chess tournaments will have to be postponed because of a steel shortage.

QUEEN'S INDIAN DEFENSE

Warsaw, 1935

[After 14 KR–K1]

WHITE	BLACK
S. Tartakover	L. Steiner
1 P–Q4	Kt–KB3
2 Kt–KB3	P–K3
3 P–KKt3	P–QKt3
4 B–Kt2	B–Kt2
5 O–O	B–K2
6 P–B4	O–O
7 Kt–B3	P–Q4
8 Kt–K5!	Q–B1 [a]
9 P×P	P×P
10 Q–Kt3	P–B3
11 B–Q2	Kt–R3? [b]
12 QR–B1	Kt–B2
13 P–K4!	R–Q1 [c]

14 KR–K1*	P–B4 [d]
15 QP×P	KtP×P [e]
16 P×P [f]	Kt(2)×P
17 B–Kt5!	R–Kt1 [g]
18 QB×Kt	B×B
19 Kt×P!	P–B5 [h]
20 Kt×R!	Resigns [i]

[116]

[a] The annoying pin contains many trappy possibilities, thus: 8 ... QKt–Q2; 9 P×P, Kt×Kt?; 10 P–Q6!, B×B; 11 P×B, Q×KP; 12 P×Kt, B×R; 13 P×Kt with two pieces for a Rook; or 8 ... P–B3; 9 P–K4, QKt–Q2?; 10 Kt×QBP!, B×Kt; 11 KP×P, B–Kt2; 12 P–Q6!

[b] 11 ... QKt–Q2 should have been tried.

[c] Black's difficulties are mounting. If 13 ... P×P; 14 Kt×KP, P–B4; 15 Kt×Kt*ch*, B×Kt (or 15 ... P×Kt; 16 B×B, Q×B; 17 Kt–Q7, KR–Q1; 18 P×P!); 16 B×B, Q×B; 17 Kt–Q7, KR–Q1; 18 P×P! with a winning game.

[d] Opening up the lines is dangerous; but White was threatening 15 P×P, KKt×P; 16 B×Kt, Kt×B (if 16 ... P×B; 17 Kt–Kt5, B–Q3; 18 Kt–B6! and wins); 17 Kt×Kt, R×Kt; 18 Kt×QBP! etc.

[e] If 15 ... B×P; 16 B–Kt5 is embarrassing.

[f] If now 16 ... Kt(3)×P; 17 Kt×Kt, Kt×Kt; 18 B–R5!, R–Q3; 19 Kt–Q3 and Black must lose some material.

[g] A clever reply: he hopes for 18 QB×Kt, B×B; 19 Kt× Kt, QB×Kt. But Tartakover will have the last laugh!

[h] The move Steiner relied on. If instead 19 ... K×Kt; 20 Kt×Kt, B×Kt; 21 B×B*ch*, K–B1; 22 Q–KB3, R×P; 23 Q–R5! and wins (23 ... Q–Q2; 24 B–K6). And if 19 ... R–Q2; 20 Kt×Kt!, B×Kt (or 20 ... R×Kt [B2]; 21 Kt–K7ch, B×Kt; 22 R×B winning); 21 B×B!, R×Q; 22 Kt–Q6*ch*, K–B1; 23 Kt×Q and wins!

[i] If 20 ... P×Q; 21 R–K8 *mate.* Or 20 ... B×Kt (Q1); 21 Q–Kt5! winning easily. Try that on your automaton!

DIAMOND CUT DIAMOND

IT IS UNIVERSALLY AGREED that brilliant games are the most enjoyable feature of chess. But where, as in Morphy's games, one of the adversaries is hopelessly outclassed, such games can come to have a disagreeably cloying effect. It is the merit of the great modern masters that they have provided us with an altogether different kind of spectacle: a bitterly contested struggle between Titans. The thrilling game which follows has been well described as "a meteor that flashes across the sky." In Botvinnik's wonderfully resourceful play we have another example of those durable qualities of the Dragon Variation which were mentioned on page 102.

SICILIAN DEFENSE
Nottingham, 1936

WHITE	BLACK
A. Alekhine	M. Botvinnik

[After 14 B–B5!]

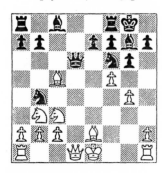

	WHITE	BLACK
1	P–K4	P–QB4
2	Kt–KB3	P–Q3
3	P–Q4	P×P
4	Kt×P	Kt–KB3
5	Kt–QB3	P–KKt3
6	B–K2	B–Kt2
7	B–K3	Kt–B3
8	Kt–Kt3	B–K3
9	P–B4	O–O
10	P–Kt4!? [a]	P–Q4!
11	P–B5!	B–B1!
12	KP×P	Kt–Kt5
13	P–Q6! [b]	Q×P!! [c]

	WHITE	BLACK
14	B–B5! [d]*	Q–B5!!
15	R–KB1 [e]	Q×RP
16	B×Kt [f]	Kt×P! [g]
17	B×Kt [h]	Q–Kt6ch
18	R–B2 [i]	Q–Kt8ch
	Drawn [j]	

[a] With this aggressive move, White announces that he is out for blood.

[b] If 13 P×P, RP×P; 14 B–B3, Kt×KtP!; 15 B×Kt, B×B; 16 Q×B, Kt×Pch with a good attack.

[c] Far better, of course, than 13 ... KP×P?; 14 P–QR3!, Kt–B3; 15 P–Kt5, Kt–K1; 16 P–B6 with a winning position.

[d] Apparently the winning move, for if now 14 ... Q×Qch (what else?!); 15 R×Q, Kt–B3 (not 15 ... Kt×Pch?; 16 K–Q2 and the foolhardy Knight pays with his life!); 16 P–Kt5, Kt–Q2; 17 P–B6, B–R1; 18 B–R3!, R–K1; 19 Kt–Q5 and Black must lose the exchange.

[e] Wins a piece—but not the game!

[f] If 16 B×P, Black has the same reply as in the text.

[g] What's another piece between friends?!

[h] 17 B–B5 is most convincingly refuted by 17 ... Q–Kt6ch; 18 B–B2, Kt×B; 19 R×Kt, B×P with a tremendous attack.

[i] Despite his two pieces plus, White is happy to take a draw: if 18 K–K2?, Q×Bch wins, or if 18 K–Q2?, B–R3ch etc.

[j] One of the greatest fighting games on record.

ODDS-GIVING IN THE
MODERN MANNER

T HE OLD MASTERS often gave odds to encourage their
hopelessly outclassed opponents. The contemporary form
of odds-giving is the simultaneous exhibition, which is
suited to modern notions of mass entertainment. The play
is on even material terms, but the master is nevertheless hand-
icapped by the physical effort of walking several miles; by
having seconds instead of minutes in which to plan and execute;
by having to rely on routine rather than on imagination. The
combination of these factors increases the possibility of blunders.

QUEEN'S GAMBIT
DECLINED

Orebro, 1937
(Simultaneous Exhibition)

[After 18 P–R3]

WHITE	BLACK
R. *Fine*	*Allies*
1 P–Q4	Kt–KB3
2 P–QB4	P–B3
3 Kt–QB3	P–Q4
4 Kt–B3	P×P
5 P–QR4	B–B4
6 Kt–K5	QKt–Q2
7 Kt×P(4)	Q–B2
8 P–KKt3	P–K4
9 P×P	Kt×P
10 B–B4	KKt–Q2
11 Q–Kt3? [a]	B–K3! [b]
12 P–K3	Kt–B6ch
13 K–Q1 [c]	Q–Q1! [d]

14 K–B1	Kt–B4
15 Q–Q1	Q×Qch
16 K×Q	O–O–Och
17 K–K2	B–Kt5 [e]
18 P–R3 [f]*	R–Q7ch!!!
19 Kt×R	Kt–Q5ch
20 K–K1	Kt–B7 *mate!* [g]

[a] An experiment which turns out badly. The "book" move 11 B–Kt2 leaves White with a comfortable game.

[b] This pin forces the following frightful weakening move (if 12 B–Kt2??, Q–B1 and wins).

[c] Likewise after 13 K–K2, Kt(6)–K4 White has a miserable position.

[d] Threatening ... Kt–B4ch.

[e] Black's game is so superior that even the exchange of Queens did not ease the pressure very much.

[f] Or 18 B–Kt2, Kt–K4ch; 19 P–B3, Kt×Kt; 20 P×B, R–Q7ch winning easily. The text allows a problem-like finish.

[g] A splendid game by the Allies (Pettersson and Ekelund).

THE HEAT OF THE BATTLE

REPULSING THREATS IS SECOND NATURE to the great master. By the time he has reached the heights in international play, he is able to parry threats almost automatically: he provides against them generally long before they arise. Such defensive mastery is an art we do not always appreciate: we do not concern ourselves overmuch with possibilities which remain in the limbo of "what might have been." But when the master, hounded by time pressure and excitement, blunders badly in the heat of the battle, he creates sensations which are enshrined in chess history.

BISHOP'S GAMBIT

Birmingham, 1937

*[After 18 Q–R5!]

	WHITE	BLACK
	J. Silverman	E. Eliskases
1	P–K4	P–K4
2	P–KB4	P×P
3	B–B4	Kt–KB3
4	Kt–QB3	P–B3
5	Kt–B3	P–Q4 [a]
6	P×P	P×P
7	B–Kt3	B–Q3
8	O–O [b]	O–O
9	P–Q4	B–K3
10	Kt–K5	B×Kt [c]
11	P×B	Q–Kt3ch
12	K–R1	Kt–Kt5
13	Q–K2 [d]	P–Q5
14	Kt–Q5	B×Kt
15	B×B	Kt–K6
16	B×Kt	QP×B [e]
17	R×P	Kt–B3
18	Q–R5! [f]*	Q×P??
19	B×Pch	K–R1 [g]
20	Q×Pch!!	Resigns [h]

[a] Logical play. As we know, the basic idea of the King's Gambit is combined attack on KB7 along the KB file and on the diagonal QB4–KB7. Black tries to keep both of these lines closed.

[b] Concentrating on development, both players are indifferent to the fate of Black's QP.

[c] Initiating a faulty plan whose end-results will be the opening up of White's attacking lines.

[d] Interestingly enough, 13 Kt×P was possible, for if 13 ... Kt–B7ch; 14 R×Kt, Q×R; 15 Kt–B7 etc.

[e] And not 16 ... BP×B?; 17 R×P!, R×R; 18 R–KB1 with a winning game. The consequences of Eliskases' dangerous inconsistency are now beginning to be evident.

[f] Black's last move is the one he relied on, hoping for 18 R–K4?, Kt×P!; 19 R×Kt, Q×P etc.
However, 18 Q–R5! sets Black a problem which he cannot solve successfully: 18 ... P–Kt3; 19 Q–R6, Q×P (else R–KR4 crushes him); 20 QR–KB1, P–K7 (if 20 ... Kt×P; 21 R–KR4. If 20 ... Q×KP; 21 R×P, R×R; 22 R×R, Q–R8ch; 23 R–B1ch and wins); 21 R×P!, R×R (if 21 ... P×R[Q]ch; 22 R×Qch, K–R1; 23 R×Rch and mate next move); 22 R×R, P–K8(Q)ch; 23 R–B1ch, K–R1; 24 R×Q and White should win (if 24 ... Kt×P; 25 Q–Kt5!, Kt–Q2; 26 Q–K7, Q–B6; 27 R–KB1 etc.).

[g] Or 19 ... R×B; 20 Q×Rch and mate in two.

[h] For if 20 ... K×Q; 21 R–R4 mate! Black's unsound plan has been refuted in splendid style.

〔123〕

TRIUMPH OF THE UNDERDOG

F OR MANY YEARS, theorists have discussed the value of the first move. Some have held that it constitutes an advantage which Black should not be able to neutralize; others feel that the first move has some utility, but not enough to prevent Black from equalizing with careful play. It was left for the brilliant young Breyer to pronounce that the first move was a disadvantage, presumably on the ground that White has to commit himself!

At any rate, we are accustomed to thinking of Black as the underdog. For that reason, it is always thrilling to see Black seize the initiative and triumph by means of a smashing attack.

NIMZOINDIAN DEFENSE

Jurata, 1937

[After 13 P–R3]

	WHITE	BLACK
	N.	A.
	Schaechter	Woitsekovsky
1	P–Q4	Kt–KB3
2	P–QB4	P–K3
3	Kt–QB3	B–Kt5
4	Q–B2	Kt–B3
5	Kt–B3	O–O
6	B–Kt5	R–K1
7	P–QR3	B×Kt*ch*
8	Q×B [a]	Q–K2 [b]
9	B–R4	P–Q3 [c]
10	P–KKt4?	P–K4!
11	P–Q5	P–K5! [d]
12	Kt–Q2	Kt–K4! [e]

13	P–R3*	Kt×QP!!
14	B×Q [f]	Kt×Q
15	B×P [g]	Kt–Q6*ch*!!
16	P×Kt	P×P*ch*
17	Kt–K4 [h]	P–Q7*ch*!!!
	Resigns [i]	

[a] The natural way to recapture, but problems will soon arise regarding the possibility of ... Kt–K5.

[b] Black has aimed at quick development. He now "threatens" ... Kt–K5. If played at once, it would have lost a Pawn.

[c] Anticipating pleasant prospects after 10 P–K3, P–K4; 11 B–K2, B–Kt5. White avoids this by the desperate measure of compromising his position.

[d] Seizing the initiative. If now 12 B×Kt, P×B!; 13 P×Kt, P×Kt; 14 Q×P(B3), P×P; 15 Q×QBP, R–Kt1 threatening ... R×P in addition to ... B–Kt2.

[e] Sharp! If now 13 Kt×P?, Kt×Kt and Black wins a piece. If 13 P–Kt5, Kt–R4; 14 Kt×P?, Kt–Kt3 again winning a piece. Or 13 B×Kt, Q×B; 14 Kt×P, Q–B5; 15 P–B3, Kt×KtP with a winning game.

[f] So the discovered attack turned up after all! If 14 P×Kt, Q×B; 15 Q×P, Kt×P or 15 ... P–K6 winning easily. White therefore gets rid of the Queens.

[g] He fights to maintain material equality, for after 15 P×Kt, R×B; 16 B–Kt2, B–K3; 17 B×P, P–QB3 Black wins easily.

[h] Hoping to be let off with 17 ... Kt×Kt (if 17 ... R×Ktch; 18 K–Q2); 18 B–B4, Kt–Kt6ch; 19 B–K3, Kt×R; 20 K–Q2. But even then 20 ... B–Q2! would save the piece (21 B–Kt2, Kt×P!). Instead, he gets a stinging surprise.

[i] He must come out a piece down.

CRIME AND PUNISHMENT

I N CHESS THE INITIATIVE IS VITAL; and yet it is more elusive than quicksilver. Worse yet, the passing of the initiative is often imperceptible. In such cases, the consequences are all the more drastic. In the following example, we see once more how Black whips up an apparently stodgy French formation into a crescendo of attacking fury.

FRENCH DEFENSE   *[After 12 ... B×P!]*

Jurata, 1937

WHITE	BLACK
Yagielsky	*A. Woitsekovsky*
1 P–K4	P–K3
2 P–Q4	P–Q4
3 Kt–QB3	Kt–KB3
4 B–Kt5	B–K2
5 B×Kt [a]	B×B
6 P–K5	B–K2
7 Q–Kt4	O–O
8 Kt–B3? [b]	P–KB4 [c]
9 Q–R3	P–B4!
10 Kt–K2? [d]	Q–R4ch!
11 P–B3	Kt–B3
12 P×P	B×P! [e]*
13 Kt–B1	B×Pch! [f]

14 K×B	Q–Kt3ch [g]
15 K–Kt3	Kt×P!!
16 Kt×Kt [h]	Q–K6ch
Resigns [i]	

[a] This antique, a prime favorite with the immortal Anderssen, has been refurbished in recent years with "the new look."

[b] A three-fold mistake: (1) he deprives the KP of support by P–B4; (2) he omits the important attacking move B–Q3; (3) he cuts off the Queen from contact with the Queen-side.

[c] A brain-teaser for White. If he captures in passing, he frees Black's game; if he retreats his Queen, he blocks a useful avenue of attack.

[d] Much too dilatory. 10 O–O–O was relatively better, although Black would have little to fear.

[e] With this offer of a piece, Black pitilessly demonstrates that the initiative is firmly in his hands. If now 13 P–QKt4, Kt×KtP; 14 P×Kt, B×KtP*ch*; 15 K–Q1, Q–R5*ch*; 16 K–B1, B–Q2 and White's King is not long for this world.

[f] A magnificent surprise.

[g] So that if 15 K–K1, Q×P; 16 Kt–Kt3, Q×P*ch* coming out with four Pawns and a tremendous attack for the sacrificed piece.

[h] Resignation: if instead 16 Kt–Kt3, P–B5*ch*; 17 K–R4, Q–Q1*ch!*; 18 K–R5 (or 18 Kt–Kt5, P–KR3), P–Kt3*ch*; 19 K–R6, Kt–B2 *mate!*

[i] If 17 Kt–B3 (on 17 K–R4, Q–B5*ch*; 18 P–Kt4 or 18 Kt–Kt4, R–B3 forces mate), P–B5*ch*; 18 K–R4, P–K4*!*; 19 P–Kt4, P×P *e.p.* wins at once (20 Q×P, Q–R3 *mate!*).

STOP! LOOK! LISTEN!

POSITION PLAY, be it ever so profound, often affects the amateur like an anesthetic. And no wonder!—for strategical plans generally require many moves in which to mature. The "inevitability of gradualness" can pall very easily. But positions that are ripe for combinative play are like unstable chemical compounds which are likely to blow up without a moment's notice. Hence their surprise qualities, making it possible, in this instance, for a master of international renown to lose in 13 moves!

PHILIDOR'S DEFENSE   *[After 11 P–B3]*

Paris, 1937

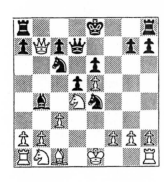

WHITE	BLACK
O. Bernstein	S. Tartakover

1	P–K4	P–K4
2	Kt–KB3	P–Q3 [*a*]
3	P–Q4	Kt–KB3
4	P×P	Kt×P
5	B–QB4	B–K3 [*b*]
6	B×B	P×B
7	Q–K2 [*c*]	P–Q4
8	Q–Kt5*ch* [*d*]	Kt–B3 [*e*]
9	Kt–Q4 [*f*]	Q–Q2
10	Q×KtP [*g*]	B–Kt5*ch*! [*h*]
11	P–B3*	Kt×Kt!!

12	Q×R*ch* [*i*]	K–B2
13	Q×R	Q–Kt4!! [*j*]
	Resigns	

[a] Who would expect Black to devise a brilliancy on a grand scale from this slow-poke opening?

[b] 5 ... P–QB3 is the safer (and less enterprising) parry to the threatened 6 B × P*ch.*

[c] The game is already in a critical stage. White attacks the Knight, and also keeps an eye on Q–Kt5*ch* winning a Pawn. Black cannot neutralize both threats; he does not need to.

[d] Tempting fate—and a very unkind one at that.

[e] With sardonic visions of this delectable possibility: 9 Q × KtP, Kt–Kt5; 10 Q–Kt5*ch*, P–B3; 11 Q–R4 (all's safe, he hopes), Kt–B4*!!* and White loses his Queen!

[f] Intensifying the pin and keeping the QKtP under threat; but Tartakover finds an inspired counter.

[g] 10 Kt × Kt would leave him hopelessly behind in development. In any event, he would rather lose the game quickly than lose face slowly.

[h] Intending the sacrifice of *both* Rooks. White has no good reply.

[i] Throwing himself on his sword, since the prosaic 12 P × B, O–O is clearly won for Black.

[j] The joker: White cannot stop mate.

TO TAKE OR NOT TO TAKE

No SELF-RESPECTING CHESS PLAYER likes to decline a
sacrifice if he honestly feels that it can be refuted. But
the problem is often complicated by time pressure,
oversights and blunders, not to mention that feeling of depression
which often sets in when defensive play seems an unwelcome
chore.

Then there are cases of over-confidence, as in the following
game, where the strength of a sacrifice is not fully appreciated.
Here general principles can help us: White's King is exposed,
his development is backward; ergo, the sacrifice should be
declined!

FOUR KNIGHTS' GAME

Hastings, 1938–39

[After 12 ... P×P!]

WHITE	BLACK
T. H.	*P. S.*
Tylor	*Milner-Barry*

1	P–K4	P–K4	
2	Kt–KB3	Kt–QB3	
3	Kt–B3	Kt–B3	
4	B–Kt5	Kt–Q5	
5	B–R4	B–B4!?	
6	Kt×P	O–O	
7	Kt–Q3 [a]	B–Kt3	
8	P–K5	Kt–K1	
9	Kt–Q5 [b]	P–Q3	
10	P–QB3	Q–R5! [c]	
11	Kt–K3	Q–K5	
12	Kt–Kt4	P×P! [d]*	
13	P×Kt [e]	P×P	
14	Q–B2	Q–K4 [f]	
15	P–B4?	Q×P!	
16	Kt–B4	Q–R5ch [g]	
17	K–B1	P–Q6! [h]	
18	Kt×P	B–KB4! [i]	
19	Kt×B	RP×Kt	
20	B–Kt3 [j]	R–Q1	
21	*Resigns* [k]		

[*a*] Awkward, but on normal-looking moves such as 7 P–Q3 or Kt–B3, P–Q4! gives Black a fine game. The Pawn sacrifice is well-suited to Milner-Barry's dashing style.

[*b*] He should assure the safety of his King with 9 O–O, although after 9 ... P–Q3; 10 P×P, Kt×QP Black's initiative is worth the Pawn.

[*c*] The first unpleasant surprise!—after 11 P×Kt (or 11 Kt×B?, Q–K5ch with considerable advantage), Q–K5ch wins a Knight advantageously.

[*d*] A second offer of a piece which has to be calculated very accurately.

[*e*] If 13 P–Q3, Q–Kt3; 14 P×Kt, P×P; 15 Kt–B4, Q×KtP; 16 R–B1, B–R6; 17 Q–K2, Kt–B3 followed by 18 ... KR–K1 with a winning game.

[*f*] White should now return the piece by castling, when the extra Pawn will be balanced by his weak Pawn position and inferior development.

[*g*] Black is a piece down, but he has a winning attack (if 17 K–Q1??, B–Kt5 *mate*!—or 17 P–Kt3, Q–K2ch regaining the piece.

[*h*] This pretty move wins even more rapidly than 17 ... Q–B3ch; 18 K–K1 (18 K–Kt1??, P–Q6ch!), Q–K2ch regaining the piece.

[*i*] Threatening 19 ... B×Ktch and 20 ... Q–B7 *mate*. If 19 P–KKt3, Q–K5 is decisive.

[*j*] If 20 B×Kt, KR×B and White is helpless. Or 20 B–Kt5, P–QB3; 21 B–B4, P–QKt4; 22 B–Kt3, R–Q1 etc.

[*k*] If 21 B–B4, Kt–Q3! (even 21 ... Q×B wins!) is crushing. A very pleasing game.

A ROSE BY ANY OTHER NAME

ONE OF THE CHESS WORLD'S perennial controversies centers about the following problem: should openings and variations be named after their founders, or after the men who first bring out the fine points in a given line of play? It is a nice question, requiring the judgment of a Solomon: a decision either way inevitably involves injustice to one party or the other.

What we now call the Colle System was for many years an obscure, anonymous and conservative variation of the Queen's Pawn Game. Hence no problem of nomenclature is involved. The dashing Belgian made of it one of the most feared attacking weapons in the whole opening repertoire.

COLLE SYSTEM
New York State
Championship, 1940

[After 14 ... P–KR3]

	WHITE	BLACK
	I. Chernev	E. S. Jackson
1	P–Q4	P–Q4
2	Kt–KB3	Kt–KB3
3	P–K3	P–K3
4	B–Q3	B–Q3
5	QKt–Q2	O–O
6	O–O	QKt–Q2
7	Q–K2 [a]	P–B4
8	P–B3	P–K4
9	P–K4	KP×P [b]
10	BP×P	QP×P
11	Kt×P	Kt×Kt?
12	Q×Kt	Kt–B3
13	Q–R4 [c]	P×P
14	B–KKt5	P–KR3 [d]*
15	B×P!	P×B
16	Q×RP	R–K1
17	QR–K1 [e]	B–K3 [f]
18	Kt–Kt5	B–KB5 [g]
19	R×B!	Resigns [h]

[132]

[a] White's immediate objective is to advance his King's Pawn, opening up the game and preparing for a King-side attack.

[b] 9 ... R–K1 was far better.

[c] The typical motif of the Colle attacking formation (mating threat at KR7) has already appeared.

[d] The threat was of course 15 B×Kt, Q×B; 16 Q×P *mate*.

[e] Not 17 KR–K1?, R×Rch; 18 R×R, B–B1!; 19 Q–Kt5ch, B–Kt2 and Black can defend himself. But 17 Kt–Kt5! would have assured White an easy win.

[f] He could have put up a real fight with 17 ... R×R necessitating 18 Q–Kt5ch!:
I   18 ... K–B1; 19 R×R, B–K3; 20 R×B!!, P×R; 21 Q–R6ch, K–Kt1; 22 Kt–Kt5!, Q–K2; 23 B–B4!, Kt–Q4; 24 Q–Kt6ch!, Q–Kt2; 25 Q×Pch, K–R1; 26 Kt–B7ch, K–Kt1; 27 Kt×Bch and wins. Or 21 ... K–K1; 22 B–Kt5ch, Kt–Q2; 23 Q–Kt6ch, K–B1 (if 23 ... K–K2; 24 Q–Kt7ch, K–K1; 25 Kt–Kt5!, Q–K2; 26 Q–Kt8ch!, Q–B1; 27 Q–Kt6ch! and wins); 24 Kt–Kt5 and wins.
II 18 ... K–R1; 19 R×R, B–K2 (if 19 ... B–B1; 20 R–K4, B–KKt5; 21 Kt–K5 and wins. Or 19 ... B–K3; 20 Q–R6ch, K–Kt1; 21 R×B!! winning as above); 20 Q–R6ch, K–Kt1; 21 R–K5, Kt–Kt5; 22 Q–R7ch and mate next move.

[g] Hoping for 19 B–R7ch, K–R1; 20 B–Kt6ch (if 20 R×B, B×Kt!), K–Kt1; 21 R×B, B×Kt!; 22 R×Rch, Q×R! But White has a quick win.

[h] If 19 ... B×Kt; 20 Q×Bch wins the Knight. If 19 ... P×R or 19 ... R×R; 20 B–R7ch and mate in two more moves. A pretty little game.

SACRIFICING THE QUEEN

For most players, the glamor of a Queen sacrifice is irresistible. This attitude is easy to understand. Tarrasch was one of the many authorities who have made the amusing observation that when an inexperienced player is confronted with mate or loss of the Queen, he prefers to be mated.

The Queen is incomparably the strongest force on the chessboard. Our respect for the Queen sacrifice is therefore a genuine tribute to the creative genius of combination, so well described by Reti as the triumph of mind over matter. Even when a player obtains more than adequate compensation for the Queen, we still experience a feeling of awe.

GRUENFELD DEFENSE
Amsterdam, 1940

[After 8]...[B–K3]

	WHITE	BLACK
	H. Kmoch	L. Prins
1	P–Q4	Kt–KB3
2	P–QB4	P–KKt3
3	Kt–QB3	P–Q4
4	Kt–B3	B–Kt2
5	Q–Kt3	P×P [a]
6	Q×BP	O–O
7	P–K4	P–Kt3
8	P–K5	B–K3 [b]*
9	P×Kt!	B×Q
10	P×B	K×P [c]
11	B×B	Kt–B3 [d]
12	B–K3	Kt–Kt5
13	O–O	Kt–B7

	WHITE	BLACK
14	QR–Q1	Kt×B
15	P×Kt [e]	P–QB4
16	Kt–KKt5!	P–K3 [f]
17	R×Pch!	Resigns [g]

[134]

[*a*] Black wants to be rid of the pressure; but the text is likely to result in a strong Pawn center for White.

[*b*] He does not wish to retreat the Knight, and he reckons on some such move as 9 Q–Q3, when he can play 9 ... Kt–Q4.

[*c*] If 10 ... B×B; 11 P×R(Q)*ch* and White has the material advantage of Rook and two pieces against Queen and Pawn.

[*d*] Black has Queen and Pawn for three minor pieces—a rough material equivalent. But White's pieces are more active—and that is what matters in the sequel.

[*e*] The Knight maneuver has opened up the King's Bishop file for White; yet Black's anxiety to clear off the inactive Knight against one of White's powerful Bishops is understandable enough.

[*f*] 16 ... Q–K1 is not much better (17 P×P, P×P; 18 B–Kt5, Q–B1; 19 R–Q7 etc.).

[*g*] For if 17 ... K–R3 (or 17 ... R×R; 18 Kt×P*ch* winning the Queen and remaining with a decisive material advantage); 18 R×P*ch!*, K×Kt; 19 P–R4*ch*, K–B4; 20 R–B1*ch*, K–Kt5; 21 B–K2*ch* and mate follows.

THE ODDS OF THE OPENING

A S OPENING TECHNIQUE continues to improve, it becomes
ever more dangerous to experiment with inferior
opening lines. The stronger one's opponent, the surer
the refutation.

It is true that some of the great masters make a practice of
adopting second-rate openings on occasion, in order to draw
their opponents into venturesome lines. This amounts to
giving the odds of the opening—a luxury which the ordinary
player cannot afford.

VIENNA GAME

Los Angeles, 1940
(Simultaneous Exhibition)

WHITE	BLACK
I. A. Horowitz	Amateur

[After 9 ... Kt–B3]

	WHITE	BLACK
1	P–K4	P–K4
2	Kt–QB3	Kt–QB3
3	B–B4	B–B4
4	Q–Kt4	Q–B3? [a]
5	Kt–Q5! [b]	Q×Pch
6	K–Q1	K–B1 [c]
7	Kt–R3	Q–Q5
8	P–Q3	B–Kt3 [d]
9	R–B1	Kt–B3 [e]*
10	R×Kt!	P–Q3 [f]

11	Q×Pch!!	K×Q
12	B–R6ch	K–Kt1
13	R–Kt6ch!!	RP×R
14	Kt–B6 mate [g]	

[a] This has an economical look about it, as it guards the King's Knight Pawn and attacks White's King's Bishop Pawn. Unfortunately, the Queen is immediately exposed to attack.

4 ... K–B1 is best, but 4 ... P–KKt3 has its drawbacks, as may be seen from the game Blake–Wainwright, London, 1910: 5 Q–Kt3, Kt–B3; 6 KKt–K2, P–Q3; 7 P–Q3, Kt–KR4; 8 Q–B3, O–O; 9 B–KR6, Kt–Kt2; 10 P–KR4!, B–K3; 11 Kt–Q5, B×Kt; 12 B×B, K–R1; 13 P–R5, P–KKt4; 14 Q–Kt4, P–B3; 15 P–KB4!, KP×P; 16 Kt×P, Kt–Q5; 17 Kt–Kt6ch!, P×Kt; 18 P×P, *resigns*.

[b] "Never spur a willing horse." This time White can disregard the proverb by forcing ... Q×Pch, as the points KKt2 and QB2 in Black's camp lose their protection, and the open King's Bishop file will be the highway to victory.

[c] There is nothing better.

[d] White was threatening to win the Queen with 9 P–B3. An old-time classic, Mieses–Tchigorin, Ostend, 1906, continued 8 ... P–Q3; 9 Q–R4, B×Kt; 10 Q×B, Kt–R4; 11 R–KB1, Kt×B; 12 Q–Q7!, P–KB3; 13 Kt×KBP!, Q–B7 (if 13 ... P×Kt; 14 R×Pch!); 14 R×Q, B×R; 15 Kt–R5, *resigns*.

[e] White was threatening to win at once with 10 Kt×B and 11 R×Pch.

[f] If 10 ... P×R; 11 B–R6ch, K–K1; 12 Q–Kt7 forces the game. The move actually made allows an even more drastic finish.

[g] Such are the hazards of giving the odds of the opening!

NOTHING BUT THE BEST

ONCE YOU HAVE EMBARKED on a combination, the proper continuation is the one which is most direct. This rules out alternative possibilities and diminishes the likelihood of error.

There are many instances of combinations which turned sour because a player did not go about his task in the most economical manner. In the game which follows, White handicaps himself, but his lapse is relatively minor.

QUEEN'S GAMBIT

U.S. Championship
Preliminaries, 1940

[After 7 ... B–K3??]

WHITE	BLACK
F. Reinfeld	*J. S. Battell*

	WHITE	BLACK
1	Kt–KB3	P–Q4
2	P–Q4	Kt–KB3
3	P–B4	P×P
4	P–K3	P–B4
5	B×P	P×P
6	P×P	Q–B2
7	Q–Kt3	B–K3?? [a]*
8	B×B!!	Q×Bch
9	K–K2	Q×R
10	B×Pch [b]	K–Q1 [c]
11	Q×P	Q–B8
12	Q×R!	Q×Pch

	WHITE	BLACK
13	QKt–Q2	Kt–K5 [d]
14	Q×Kt	Q×R
15	Q–Q5ch	K–B2
16	Q–B5ch	K–Q1 [e]
17	B–K6	Resigns [f]

[*a*] Black has made some bad errors of judgment. His fifth
move opened up lines prematurely for White's pieces; his
sixth move developed the Queen too soon; his seventh is
made under the mistaken impression that his Bishop
cannot be captured.

[*b*] There was a quicker win with 10 Q×P*!!* If then 10 . . .
P×B (10 . . . Q–B8; 11 Kt–B3*!*); 11 Q–B8*ch*,
K–B2; 12 Kt–K5*ch*, K–Kt1; 13 Q×P *mate!*

[*c*] With a Rook ahead, Black cannot hold the position! If
10 . . . K–Q2; 11 Q×P*ch* wins rapidly.

[*d*] Despair. If 13 . . . Q×R; 14 Q×Kt*ch*, K–Q2;
15 Kt–K5 *mate.*

[*e*] If 16 . . . K–Kt2; 17 B–K6 decides quickly.

[*f*] For if 17 . . . Kt–Q2; 18 Q–B6 (the quickest), Kt–Kt3;
19 Kt–K5 followed by Kt–B7 *mate.*

[139]

SOMETHING NEW UNDER
THE SUN

THAT WHICH HATH BEEN is that which shall be; and that which hath been done is that which shall be done; and there is no new thing under the sun." When we study the progress of combination play during the past hundred years, we see that so much has been done that we despair of new possibilities turning up. That is why we are impressed by the stunning subtlety and originality of Black's fourteenth move in this game. It is all the more shattering when contrasted with the preceding commonplace course of the game. Nimzovich would have saluted it as the most "mysterious Rook move" of them all!

GIUOCO PIANO
Rio de Janeiro, 1942

[After 14 ... R–KKt1!!!]

WHITE	BLACK
C. Gomes	C. Neto

1	P–K4	P–K4
2	Kt–KB3	Kt–QB3
3	Kt–B3	B–B4
4	B–B4	P–Q3
5	P–Q3	B–KKt5
6	B–K3	Kt–Q5! [a]
7	B×Kt	B×B
8	P–KR3	B–R4
9	Kt–QKt5? [b]	B–QKt3
10	Q–K2	Kt–K2! [c]
11	O–O	P–QR3
12	Kt–R3 [d]	Kt–Kt3! [e]
13	P–KKt3 [f]	Q–B3!

14	K–Kt2	R–KKt1!!!*
15	P–B3 [g]	Kt–R5ch!!
16	P×Kt	P–Kt4!!
17	R–KKt1	B×Ktch!
18	Q×B	P×Pch
19	Resigns [h]	

[140]

[a] Black has seized the initiative.

[b] The decentralization should (and does) turn out badly. 9 P–KKt4 was preferable, or, better yet, 9 Q–K2 followed by Kt–Q1, P–B3 and Kt–K3.

[c] The Knight is to head for KB5 via KKt3. White is reluctant to prevent this maneuver by driving back Black's Queen's Bishop with P–KKt4, as this would weaken the White Pawn structure.

[d] Apparently in the hope of later advancing in the center by P–B3, Kt–B2 and P–Q4.

[e] This does not lose a piece (13 P–KKt4, Kt–B5!).

[f] White's desire to keep out the Knight is understandable, but now the pin becomes deadly.

[g] There was no satisfactory defense. Thus if 15 Kt–QKt1, Kt–R5ch!!; 16 P×Kt, P–Kt4!!; 17 QKt–Q2, P–Kt5!; 18 P×P, R×Pch; 19 K–R3, R×Pch; 20 K–Kt3, Q–Kt3ch; 21 K×R, Q–Kt5 mate.

[h] If 19 K–R2, Q×Q; 20 R×Rch, K–K2; 21 R×R, Q×BPch; 22 K–R1, Q–B6ch; 23 K–R2, Q–Kt6ch; 24 K–R1, Q×P mate. A worthy sequel to a first-rate combination.

ONCE IN A LIFETIME

WE NATURALLY EXPECT the finest chess to be played by the great masters, and this is true of their total output when viewed at its selective best. Yet many an unknown, who has botched most of his games and ruined innumerable promising positions, succeeds at some point or other in playing the game of a lifetime. Thus he enjoys a passing moment of greatness, incidentally enriching our lives with a unique masterpiece.

*NIMZOINDIAN
DEFENSE*

Brussels, 1942

WHITE	BLACK
M. Defosse	*Frank*
1 P–Q4	Kt–KB3
2 Kt–KB3	P–K3
3 P–B4	P–QKt3
4 Kt–B3 [a]	B–Kt2
5 P–K3 [b]	B–Kt5
6 Q–B2	Kt–K5
7 B–Q3	P–KB4
8 P–QR3	B×Ktch
9 P×B	O–O
10 O–O [c]	R–B3! [d]
11 Kt–Q2	R–R3 [e]
12 P–Kt3??*	Q–R5!! [f]

[After 12 P–Kt3??]

13 Kt–B3 [g]	Kt–Kt4!!!
14 P×Q [h]	Kt×Ktch
15 K–Kt2 [i]	Kt–K8ch!!
16 K–Kt3 [j]	R–Kt3ch
17 K–B4	R–Kt5ch
18 K–K5	Kt–B6 *mate* [k]

[*a*] This game offers still another proof that 4 P–KKt3 is White's best chance of holding some initiative.

[*b*] 5 B–Kt5 is more aggressive.

[*c*] Castling into a powerful attack; but it is difficult to suggest a good alternative.

[*d*] Relying on the action of this Rook, the advanced Knight, the long-range Bishop and the Queen, Black plans a devastating attack.

[*e*] It is now absolutely essential for White to capture the Knight.

[*f*] Alertly seizing on White's lapse. If now 13 P × Q, R–Kt3*ch*; 14 K–R1, Kt × P *mate*. But the best is yet to come!

[*g*] Now Black's Queen is doubly attacked; but he has in reserve a charming sacrifice (which must be accepted) to expose the weak white squares to the raking fire of the terrible Bishop.

[*h*] Stretching out the game a bit: if 14 Kt × Q, Kt–R6 *mate*.

[*i*] A delicious finale results from 15 K–R1, R × P; 16 K–Kt2, Kt–K8*ch!*; 17 K–Kt3 (or 17 K–Kt1, R–Kt5 *mate*), R–Kt5*ch*; 18 K–R3, B–Kt7 *mate*.

[*j*] 16 K–R3, B–Kt7*ch*; 17 K–Kt3, R–Kt3*ch* loses as in the text.

[*k*] A less "brutal" finish than 18 . . . Kt–B3 *mate*.

IT TAKES TWO

ODAY WE KNOW that combinations are impossible without previous weak play on the part of one's opponent.
The steady rise in average playing strength has therefore
had the effect of decreasing the number of occasions for flashy
combinative play. A century ago, when there was only a
handful of first-rate players, the prospect for brilliant play was
much brighter.

Yet combinations are better and more numerous than they
ever were before! This is due to the fact that far more games
are played—and published. True, the last remaining contact
between master and amateur is the simultaneous performance,
and it is in precisely this field that some of the most sensational
combinations are being produced.

DANISH GAMBIT

Detroit, 1945
(Simultaneous Exhibition)

WHITE	BLACK
A. S. Denker	*Gonzalez*

*[After 18 Q–R6!!]

1	P–K4	P–K4
2	P–Q4	P×P
3	P–QB3	P×P
4	B–QB4	P×P
5	B×P [*a*]	B–Kt5*ch*
6	K–B1!? [*b*]	Kt–KB3
7	P–K5	Kt–Kt1
8	Q–Kt4	B–B1 [*c*]
9	Q–B3	Kt–KR3
10	Kt–B3	B–K2
11	Kt–Q5	O–O
12	Kt–B6*ch!*	K–R1 [*d*]

13	Kt–R3	B×Kt? [*e*]
14	P×B	P–KKt3 [*f*]
15	Q–B4!	Kt–B4
16	Kt–Kt5	Kt–Q3 [*g*]
17	Kt×P*ch!!*	Kt×Kt [*h*]
18	Q–R6!!*	*Resigns* [*i*]

[144]

[a] Black would do well now to adopt the simplifying course
5 ... P–Q4; 6 B×QP, Kt–KB3; 7 B×Pch, K×B;
8 Q×Q, B–Kt5ch; 9 Q–Q2, B×Qch with the better
endgame for Black. This is typical of the way that masters
use small-scale combinations to avert grand combinations.

[b] Avoids simplifying combinations.

[c] Not 8 ... P–Q4?; 9 B–Kt5ch! (if 9 Q×P?, P×B;
10 Q×R?, Q–Q8 mate), P–B3; 10 Q×P etc.

[d] Or 12 ... P×Kt; 13 P×P, B–Q3; 14 Q–R5 with a
winning game.

[e] 13 ... P–Q3 was a better defensive try.

[f] The attempt to close the diagonal is doomed to disappoint-
ment.

[g] Apparently holding everything.

[h] Equally brilliant play would ensue on 17 ... R×Kt;
18 B×R, Kt×B; 19 Q–R6!!, Q–Kt1 (if 19 ...
Kt×Q; 20 P–B7ch leads to mate); 20 R–K1! and
Black is helpless against 21 R–K8!

[i] Black sees that after 18 ... R–Kt1 (not 18 ... Kt×Q;
19 P–B7ch and mate follows); 19 B×Kt (threatening
20 Q–Kt7ch!) he would have no defense: 19 ... Q–B1;
20 B–Q5!!, Q×Q; 21 P–B7ch and mate next move!
Note that all of Black's Queen-side pieces are still at
home!

"A LITTLE LEARNING IS A DANGEROUS THING"

ONE OF THE THORNS on the road to chess mastery is the fact that knowledge is acquired at the cost of spontaneity. Many a reader who has relished this dour aphorism has thoughtlessly accepted the implication that a great deal of learning is necessarily beneficial.

It does not always work out like that. There are masters who are reputed to know thousands of opening variations by heart—and this includes the citations, parentheses and brackets. Their knowledge is broad but not deep; extensive but not intensive. When they try to be original, they falter against younger players who, lacking their learning, have a flair for colorful combinative play.

SICILIAN DEFENSE

Vienna, 1946

WHITE	BLACK
K. Galia	E. Gruenfeld

1	P–K4	P–QB4
2	Kt–KB3	Kt–QB3
3	P–Q4	P×P
4	Kt×P	Kt–B3
5	Kt–QB3	P–K4? [a]
6	Kt(4)–Kt5	P–Q3
7	P–QR4 [b]	P–QR3
8	Kt–R3	B–K3 [c]
9	B–B4	B×B
10	Kt×B	Kt×P? [d]
11	Kt×Kt	P–Q4 [e]*
12	B–Kt5!!!	P–B3 [f]

*[After 11 ... P–Q4]

13	B×P!	P×B
14	Q×P!! [g]	B–K2
15	Kt(K4)–Q6ch	B×Kt [h]
16	Kt×Bch	K–K2
17	O–O–O	Kt–Q5
18	R×Kt!	Resigns [i]

[a] This move is frowned upon by the theorists, for it leaves a backward Queen's Pawn and a hole at Black's Q4.

[b] Or 7 B–Kt5, P–QR3; 8 B×Kt, P×B; 9 Kt–R3, P–Kt4; 10 Kt–Q5 with a fine game for White.

[c] A tense struggle is in the offing. Black wants to force ... P–Q4, thus ridding himself of the weak Pawn. This explains White's reply.

[d] A neat combination, which wins . . . for White!

[e] Regaining the piece and getting rid of the weakness. But there is a stunning surprise.

[f] Petition in bankruptcy. However, on 12 ... B–K2 or 12 ... Kt–K2 White checks at Q6 with an easy win.

[g] The icing on the cake. If now 14 ... Q×Q; 15 Kt×Pch coming out two Pawns ahead.

[h] 15 ... K–B1 allows mate on the move. 15 ... K–Q2 loses the Queen.

[i] For if 18 ... P×Kt; 19 R–K1ch winning as in the previous note. A frolicsome affair.

MAKING SOMETHING OUT
OF NOTHING

THERE IS ONE TYPE of combination which is never considered in the chess manuals: the combination which, though sound, is superfluous. Chess writers take it for granted that if a sacrifice can be declined without disadvantage, one's opponent will "naturally" do the "sensible" thing.

The annotator is concerned only with what can be analyzed objectively. In over-the-board play, however, "non-analytical" factors play a great role: the bluff, the dare, the gamble, the "swindle" and the trap cannot be completely analyzed variation-wise.

PETROFF DEFENSE

Correspondence, 1946

WHITE	BLACK
J. C. Rather	A. Sandrin

*[After 15 ... P × B]

1 P–K4	P–K4		
2 Kt–KB3	Kt–KB3		
3 Kt × P	P–Q3		
4 Kt–KB3	Kt × P		
5 P–Q4	P–Q4		
6 B–Q3	B–Q3		
7 O–O	B–KKt5		
8 P–B4	P–QB3 [a]		
9 QKt–Q2	Kt × Kt [b]	14 R × Bch	K–B2
10 R–K1ch!! [c]	Kt–K5 [d]	15 P–Q5!	P × B [h]*
11 B × Kt	P × B? [e]	16 P × P!!	P × P [i]
12 R × Pch	B–K3 [f]	17 R × B	Q–R4
13 B–Kt5!	P–B3 [g]	18 P–B5!	Resigns [j]

[148]

[a] Not quite satisfactory, for White has a troublesome pin
with 9 R–K1: 9 ... P–KB4; 10 Kt–B3!, B–B2;
11 Kt×Kt!, BP×Kt; 12 B×P, P×B; 13 R×P*ch*
and wins; or 10 ... B–K2; 11 Q–Kt3 and Black has
no good move.

[b] Expecting 10 B×Kt, P×P; 11 R–K1*ch*, B–K2;
12 B×BP, O–O with a good game.

[c] A very fine move requiring hair-sharp calculation.

[d] Black accepts the dare. Devotees of the simple life would
prefer 10 ... B–K2 etc. as above.

[e] 11 ... O–O was in order (12 P×P, P×P; 12 B×P,
B×P*ch* etc.). But he can hardly be blamed for not seeing
the whole point of White's combination.

[f] Confidently awaiting 13 P–Q5, which he will answer
with 13 ... O–O! so that if 14 P×B??, B×P*ch*!

[g] Still trying to hold on to the extra piece!

[h] His position is apparently quite safe, though a bit uncomfortable.

[i] Against 16 ... K×R Rather had planned 17 Q–Q5*ch*,
K–K2; 18 R–K1*ch*, K–B1; 19 P×P and wins; or
16 ... B×P*ch*; 17 K×B, Q×Q; 18 Kt×P*ch*!!,
K–B1; 19 P×P!, Q–R4*ch* (if 19 ... Q×R; 20 P×R
[Q], Q×KtP; 21 Q–B3*ch* with a quick mate); 20
K–Kt1 and wins!

[j] If 18 ... Q×BP; 19 Q–Kt3*ch* with crushing effect;
or 18 ... R–K1; 19 Kt×P*ch*, K–Kt1; 20 Q–Kt3*ch*,
K–R1 and our old friend Philidor's Legacy turns up:
21 Kt–B7*ch*, K–Kt1; 22 Kt–R6*ch*, K–R1; 23 Q–
Kt8*ch*! etc.

"WHAT'S HE UP TO?!"

THERE IS ONE RESPECT in which chess differs from the other arts: the player who wants to create a masterpiece is both hindered and helped by his opponent. It is the presence of this living, refractory material that makes chess as difficult as it is fascinating.

At all times we must take thought about our adversary: "What's he up to?!" We may use variation analysis, scholastic reasoning, psychology, telepathy, divination, crystal-gazing, fortune-telling, augury, "swindling," or just plain guessing. But we must never forget that the opponent has a mind and will of his own: we must never confuse him with the chess pieces.

QUEEN'S GAMBIT
DECLINED

World Correspondence
Championship, 1947

[After 13 ... Kt × KP?]

WHITE	BLACK
B. *Wikstrom*	B. H. *Wood*

1	P–Q4	P–Q4
2	P–QB4	P–K3
3	Kt–QB3	Kt–KB3
4	B–Kt5	QKt–Q2
5	Kt–B3	P–B3
6	P×P [*a*]	KP×P
7	P–K3	B–K2
8	B–Q3	O–O
9	O–O	R–K1
10	Q–B2	P–KR3
11	B×Kt [*b*]	Kt×B [*c*]
12	Kt–K5	Kt–Kt5 [*d*]

13	P–B4!! [*e*]	Kt×KP?[*f*]*
14	B–R7*ch*	K–B1 [*g*]
15	Q–K2	Kt–B4 [*h*]
16	Q–R5	Kt–Q3 [*i*]
17	Q×P*ch!!*	Kt×Q
18	Kt–Kt6 *mate* [*j*]	

[150]

[a] A modish method of avoiding the Cambridge Springs Variation (6 P–K3, Q–R4).

[b] An unusual but by no means pointless deviation from the customary B–KB4 or B–R4.

[c] 11 ... B × B gives a more comfortable game.

[d] He naturally seeks exchanges in order to neutralize any attacking possibilities, and also to make his two Bishops tell.

[e] "What's he up to?!" The move leaves a Pawn and the exchange *en prise*, so it "must" be a blunder. Perhaps not. . . .

[f] Black's diagnosis: his opponent's last move was a blunder.

[g] And not 14 ... K–R1??; 15 Kt × P *mate.*

[h] There was still a fighting chance with 15 ... Kt–Kt5; 16 Kt × Kt, B–QB4—for example 17 Q–B3, B × P*ch*; 18 K–R1, P–KKt3; but then 19 P–B5*!!* is decisive. Of course, if 15 ... Kt × R?; 16 Q–R5, B–K3 (if 16 ... P–KKt3??; 17 Q × P *mate*); 17 P–B5, B–Q3; 18 P × B and Black can resign.

[i] This allows an exquisite finish; but 16 ... P–KKt3; 17 B × P held out no hope for Black.

[j] A game which is as enjoyable as it is instructive. White's victory is all the more creditable in that it was achieved against one of Europe's best correspondence players.

HOMEWORK

T HIS THRILLING GAME ("only a draw") illustrates a phenomenon which is not new but has been perfected in modern times. This is the struggle between two masters who have prepared variations in the same line of play. Each master has armed himself with clever finesses in the hope of outwitting his opponent. The contest starts long before they sit down in the tournament room . . . may the best surprise win!

FRENCH DEFENSE
Vina del Mar, 1947

*[After 9 ... K–B1]

WHITE	BLACK
H. Rossetto	G. Stahlberg
1 P–K4	P–K3
2 P–Q4	P–Q4
3 Kt–QB3	Kt–KB3
4 B–Kt5	B–K2
5 P–K5	KKt–Q2
6 P–KR4	P–QB4
7 Kt–Kt5!? [a]	P–B3 [b]
8 B–Q3! [c]	P–QR3!
9 Q–R5ch!	K–B1 [d]*
10 R–R3!	P×Kt [e]
11 B–R6!! [f]	Q–R4ch [g]
12 B–Q2 [h]	Q–B2 [i]

13 R–Kt3!	P×QP! [j]
14 Kt–B3!	Kt×P
15 R×P!!	P–R3!! [k]
16 B–R7!! [l]	K×R
17 Q×Pch	Drawn [m]

[a] A highly speculative line instead of the safe and sane 7 B×B.

[b] Apparently demolishing White's center with favorable consequences, for example: 8 KP×P, Kt×P; 9 B–KB4, O–O!; 10 Kt–B7, Kt–K5! etc.

[c] So that if 8 ... P×B; 9 Q–R5ch, K–B1; 10 RP×P! (threatening 11 R–R3), B×P; 11 Kt–Q6! with a strong attack.

[d] White must now lose a piece. Where is his compensation?

[e] 10 ... P×B would not do because of 11 R–B3ch etc.

[f] According to *Modern Chess Openings* (Korn) there is a draw by 11 ... P×B; 12 Q×Pch, K–K1; 13 Q–R5ch etc. But, as Rather points out, White can win with 13 B–Kt6ch!, P×B; 14 Q×Pch!, K–B1; 15 R–KKt3 and if 15 ... Q–R4ch; 16 K–Q1.

[g] The analysts have overlooked that Black can force an immediate draw (if he wants it) with 11 ... P×B; 12 Q×Pch, K–B2! for now 13 R–Kt3? is defeated by 13 ... B–B1.

[h] Forced (12 K–Q1?, P×B; 13 Q×Pch, K–K1 and Black's King flees to the Queen-side).

[i] Spurning the draw by 12 ... Q–Q1; 13 B–R6, Q–R4ch; 14 B–Q2, Q–Q1 etc.

[j] Threatens to swap Queens.

[k] Not 15 ... K×R? (if 15 ... Kt×Ktch; 16 K–Q1!! wins); 16 B–R6ch and mate in two.

[l] Avoiding 16 B×RP?, B–Kt5ch!; 17 K–K2, Q×R; 18 B×Qch, K×B and White's Queen is lost! An even simpler refutation of 16 B×RP? is 16 ... R×B!; 17 Q×R, B–Kt5ch!

[m] Both sides must be content with the perpetual check!

INDEX OF OPENINGS

PRINTED AT THE PITMAN PRESS, BATH, SOMERSET, ENGLAND